CREATING A CUSTOMER EXPERIENCE THAT SINGS

AN INTRODUCTION TO CUSTOMER JOURNEY MAPPING FOR MARKETERS

JENNIFER L. CLINEHENS

For my parents, who have always helped me chase my dreams.

And for my partner Rob, who had the patience to listen to me talk about writing this book for a year and never doubted I'd finish it. His invaluable advice, guidance and experience helped shape this book.

Without their belief and support this book never would have been finished.

INTRODUCTION

WHY DOES CUSTOMER EXPERIENCE MATTER?

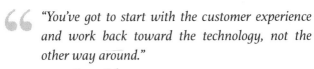 *"You've got to start with the customer experience and work back toward the technology, not the other way around."*
– Steve Jobs

It's one of the hottest topics in marketing. **Customer Experience**—much like Big Data, Marketing Automation, AI, and the Blockchain—is an area that's widely discussed but not well understood.

Thought leaders without much skin in the game tout CX as a cure-all for brands. Agencies go on hiring sprees. Marketers shuffle their org charts. It all seems so sexy—so *strategic*.

But when you get down to brass tacks, there's not a lot of clarity around the Customer Experience process, outputs and KPIs.

According to a recent study by Havas[1], 81% of brands could disappear tomorrow and customers wouldn't care. As shocking as that statistic may seem (to marketers), it's not surprising when you start digging into Customer Experience stats. A whopping 92% of customers in a Bain and Company survey[2] said that companies fail to deliver on basic CX promises.

And that's a big, high-stakes problem.

So if you're trying to fix your customer experience, where do you start? That's where the Customer Journey Map comes in.

Why I wrote this book

Although there are several excellent books on Experience Mapping, I wasn't satisfied with the available resources for marketers. Many of these books talk about Journey Mapping at a more strategic level, but not a practical one.

Given how important customer experience and Journey Mapping are to the future of marketing, I felt such a guide needed to be written.

Designed to be a jumping-off point, this book introduces the language, creation process, and uses for Customer Journey Maps. It's designed to be a quick read without a lot of fluff, just the nuts and bolts of making a Journey Map happen.

In an ideal world, you will finish this book and start creating CJMs right away, while continuing to learn from other resources and your own practice. Even though it would be a huge compliment, please don't stop here. There's a whole world of Journey Mapping content out there (a lot of which I've referenced as "Additional Resources" in this book).

The Structure of "CX That Sings"

There are three big sections in this guide - designed to help you understand the piece parts of CJMs, how to build your own, and some tips on using your map to spur partners into action.

1. **Understanding the Map:** Best practice, examples of customer journey maps, templates, and checklists to help you get from zero to completed map with as little pain as possible.

2. **Building the Map:** From the initial discovery workshop to final visualization and validation, you'll be guided through best practice examples, checklists, case studies, and common mistakes in experience mapping. Includes a section on common mental biases, working cross-functionally, and using the Journey Map to sell-in the right next steps (if you're an agency), or get support for these projects from others in your organization (if you're a product manager, brand manager, or marketing director).

3. **Using your Map:** Learn how to use this as a jumping off point to develop additional opportunities, solutions, product and experience innovations, and build relationships that get CX initiatives funded, tested, completed, and measured.

In each chapter, I've included easy-to-scan sections like **Key Terms and Definitions, What You Need to Remember, Further Reading, Links, and Additional Resources.**

A quick note on Journey Mapping

Despite what some consultancies, agencies, and thought leaders say, there's no one way to create a Journey Map. This book aims to distill fundamental guiding principals. You may find that your approach will vary slightly from mine.

That's great - you do you! But like learning to be a musician, you have to absorb the fundamentals before you can learn to improvise. Consider this guide your introduction to the notes, rhythms, and scales of Journey Mapping. Where you take the melody is up to you.

Who was this book written for?

In writing this guide, I've assumed zero prior knowledge of a wide range of subjects: advertising, communications design, behavioral psychology, qualitative research, data analysis, and design. This isn't intended to insult anyone. Instead, it's a reflection of the audience I had in mind while writing.

Although anyone should be able to read CX That Sings and hit the ground running, there are a few audiences that will benefit the most:

1. Brand-side marketers, product managers, and anyone else who needs to know about customer-first thinking

<u>Meet Jane:</u> She's a client-side marketing manager who specializes in direct communications for a large fast casual dining chain. She's in charge of creating an onboarding email campaign for the company's new mobile app.

Jane's agency suggests they put together a customer journey map to better understand the pain points these emails might address.

But Jane's a little unsure.

She has a top-tier MBA, but her marketing program didn't mention customer-focused empathy tools. Instead, her professors spent a lot of time on classic strategic frameworks like Blue Ocean, SWOT, and Porter's Five Forces.

Jane has heard of Customer Journey Mapping. She's even Googled it and seen an example or two. But she doesn't have experience in the creation process, so she's not sure what value it might provide.

The question she's asking herself is, "Why should I pay for a big, expensive piece of strategy work when we can just use common sense? Don't we already have a pretty good understanding of our customers and what they need?"

Jane will use consumer journey maps for communications planning and internal strategy development and alignment.

Her biggest challenge is, **"I've heard customer journey mapping is important... but is it valuable to me?"**

2. Agency-side strategists, planners, account folks, and consultants

<u>Meet Ben:</u> He's an agency-side strategist who wants to better understand the process of putting together a Customer Journey Map.

As his agency evolves from being digital specialists to a more experience-focused shop, Ben sees the writing on the wall. If he wants to keep up with where the agency, clients, and the industry are heading, he needs to learn more about the process of Customer Journey Mapping.

Ben will use Journey Maps for communications planning and strategy development. He'll also combine Journey

Maps with other forms of research and data to present solutions for clients.

His biggest challenge is, **"I've heard Customer Journey Mapping is important... but how do I create one, and use it to solve my clients' challenges?"**

About the Author

Jennifer Clinehens is a CX strategist who's worked both brand and agency-side across North America, Australia, Asia, the U.K., and Europe. Currently, she's the Head of Experience at The Marketing Store in London.

Her client-side experience includes time spent as an entrepreneur and Senior Manager at AT&T. Ms. Clinehens has also lent her strategic expertise to companies like Adidas, Coca-Cola, Delta Airlines, Marks and Spencer (U.K.), Westpac (AU), and McDonald's (Global).

Ms. Clinehens has studied business and marketing at institutions like the University of Virginia, Goizueta Business School at Emory University (MBA), and the prestigious Virginia Commonwealth University Brandcenter (MS).

CREATING A CUSTOMER EXPERIENCE THAT SINGS

PART I

UNDERSTANDING THE CUSTOMER JOURNEY MAP

"Your customers can tell you the things that are broken and how they want to be made happy. Listen to them. Make them happy."

  - Mark Cuban

1

THE CUSTOMER EMPATHY GAP

WHY YOU DON'T UNDERSTAND YOUR CUSTOMERS AND
WHAT TO DO ABOUT IT

 "We see our customers as invited guests to a party, and we are the hosts. It's our job every day to make every important aspect of the customer experience a little bit better."
– Jeff Bezos

Does CX Pass the ROI Test?

McKinsey & Company has performed extensive research regarding the business impact of CX. In their analysis, they've found "companies that offer consistently best-in-class customer experiences tend to grow faster and more profitably[1]."

These CX leaders are 80% more likely to retain customers, get more positive referrals, and they don't have to spend as much on marketing to drive growth. It's clear that an excellent customer experience has a direct impact on companies' bottom lines.

But if it's so important, why do so many brands get customer experience wrong?

The story that most businesses tell themselves is that they deliver a "superior experience", according to a recent Bain & Co. study[2]. Not just a good experience. A *superior* one.

After asking companies their opinions about their experience, Bain then flipped the script. They asked customers what they thought of these brands' experiences.

Only 8% of customers said these brands delivered on a *basic* customer experience.

And that's the critical issue—there's a breakdown between what brands are convinced their customers think, and what customers actually think.

It's more fundamental than what Bain calls the "delivery gap". **It's a customer empathy gap.**

Defining the Customer Empathy Gap

As soon as you join an organization, you're no longer that company's customer. You're now on a never-ending quest to find Market Orientation—the ability to see your brand from the customer's point of view.

The concept of **market orientation** means being in tune with who your customer is and what they think, feel, believe, and want. On the surface, this seems like it should be easy. But how many of you have sat through marketing meetings where one personal antidote—"me-search", if you will—overturns thousands of customer data points?

Where someone with nothing in common with the customer strategizes "from the gut"?

That would be fine and dandy if marketers were exactly like their customers. But they're not.

According to a survey by Trinity Mirror Solutions[3], marketers are more affluent, educated, left-wing, and open to risk-taking than the general public.

As someone who has worked on world-class "value brands" I can tell you that secretly lots of marketers just don't get their brand's core customers.

I've seen far too many recommendations to shift brands upmarket, rework campaigns, and invest in esoteric platforms—not because that's best for customers, but because people are marketing to themselves.

The Cognitive Bias We're All Guilty Of…

Marketers—like all humans—fall prey to the cognitive bias of **"in-group favoritism"**.

We form a specific world view, surround ourselves with an echo chamber of like-minded people, and think everyone on Earth shares the same point of view.

Because we're driven by this unconscious bias, relying on our guts in marketing is dangerous business. Marketers must make sure they're seeking out Market Orientation at every opportunity.

This is an issue you see in every industry—how you think when you're up close to a project isn't how the world views your work.

The musician and producer Brian Eno described the same effect in the music industry:

> *"You're a completely different person as a maker than you are as a listener.*
>
> *That's one of the reasons I so often leave the studio to listen to things.*
>
> *A lot of people never leave the studio when they're making something, so they're always in that maker mode, screwdriving things in—adding, adding, adding.*
>
> *Because it seems like the right thing to be doing in that room. But it's when you come out that you start to hear what you like."*
>
> —Brian Eno

It's in the never-ending quest to gain market orientation that empathy tools like the Customer Journey Map become critical.

If you don't understand your customers, how can you expect them to buy your products?

To Create Empathy, Use a Customer Journey Map

The first step to creating a breakthrough CX is created by seeing through the eyes of your customers.

That's where Customer Journey Maps come in.

Their core purpose is acting as a visual of how people experience your brand, and the pain points that keep them from coming back.

Only after understanding the experience of those who buy your products, can you hope to improve the process in a meaningful way.

≈

Key Terms

Customer Experience (CX)

The story people tell themselves about your brand, derived from their experiences with and perceptions of your brand, product, and/or service.

Customer Journey Map

A tool that helps marketers identify organize, verify, and socialize the customer experience. It also helps marketers understand what customers need by discovering gaps in the CX. We can then use these learnings to research and propose solutions to these gaps.

Market Orientation

The critical marketing skill of being in tune with who your real customer is and what they think, feel, believe, and want.

Customer Empathy Gap

The gap between what brands are convinced their customers think/feel/experience, and what customers actually think/feel/experience.

In-Group Favoritism

The tendency to lean on "in-group bias" when evaluating research, ideas, and data. Basically, we form a specific world view, surround ourselves with an echo chamber of like-minded people, and think everyone on Earth shares the same point of view.

2

THE BASICS

WHAT MAKES A KILLER CUSTOMER JOURNEY MAP

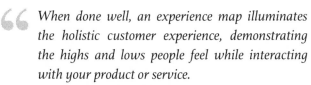 *When done well, an experience map illuminates the holistic customer experience, demonstrating the highs and lows people feel while interacting with your product or service.*

The process of mapping uncovers the key customer moments that, once improved, will unlock a more compelling and more valuable overall experience.

- Adaptive Path, "Guide to Experience Mapping"

I f you type "Customer Journey Map" into an image search, you're likely to be more confused than enlightened. Experience Mapping may have its roots in design, but since it's been adopted into the business mainstream, interest (and the number of "experts") has exploded.

The result is hundreds—maybe thousands—of boutique customer experience practices popping up and putting their proprietary spin on the basic template.

For illustration purposes, I've distilled the Customer

Journey Map into its essential elements. With a strong understanding of the fundamentals, you can iterate to your heart's content.

But for now, let's agree on a few must-haves.

The goal of a Customer Journey Map is to create a visual story about how people interact with your brand.

Journey Maps act as a bridge of understanding between the brand and the customer.

They'll help overcome the Empathy Gap described in the first chapter. Journey Maps will empower your executives to work cross-functionally and iron out all of your experience issues. The resulting CX work will increase margins and shareholder value.

But before we get too carried away with the results, let's set a few parameters for the output.

The 6 Keys to an Effective Customer Journey Map

As any framework, the specific sections and verbiage will differ from brand to brand. But if your Journey Map includes the following you're on the right track:

- Customer Persona
- Purchase journey (also known as Path to Purchase) divided into specific steps or phases
- Touchpoints customers will interact with or use during their experience
- A specific goal and the actions a customer must take to accomplish it
- Detail regarding the customer's needs, pain

points, and emotional state during each step of
their purchase journey
- Opportunities for the brand to better address
customer pain points and frustrations

**The template below is an example a basic Customer
Journey Map:**

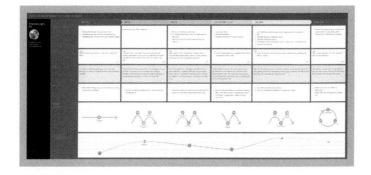

Please note: there's a full page, rotated image of this Customer Journey Map at the end of this chapter, as well as in the appendix.

You can also download a digital copy at CXThatSings.com/Resources

Taken separately, the pieces of this Journey Map aren't too helpful. They may help you improve a tactic here or there.

However, put these pieces together, and the Journey Map becomes a potent tool—giving you a peek into the real-world experience of your customers, and a high-level visual of their that holistic journey.

It's from this starting place that you can create a truly breakthrough customer experience for your brand.

A Deep Dive Into the Sections of the Customer Journey Map

1. Persona

A marketing persona is a semi-fictional representation of a group of your customers. Based on research and data from your existing customers, a persona is a heuristic that represents an essential segment of your buyers. Personas bring your customers to life through both demographic and psychographic details.

Limit Journey Maps to the experience of one persona and their path toward one primary goal. As stated earlier, the primary goal of a CJM is to bring clarity to an ambiguous buying process. If you try to capture every single customer and every journey they take in one map, you'll miss the signal in the noise.

We'll talk more about the process of creating a Persona in Chapter 3, but for now you can find an example below:

Don't forget, you can download a free version of this Persona at CXThatSings.com/Resources

2. Phases of the Purchase Journey (aka Path to Purchase)

This section outlines the high-level process customers follow from awareness to purchase, and beyond.

In real life, this isn't a linear journey, and different sections might overlap. However, for the sake of illustration, we divide the journey into discrete and step-wise parts.

In consumer brands, there tends to be 4–6 phases in a purchase journey. In practice, you may include more, less, or different phases in your map.

It all depends on your particular industry, product, and customer type.

A B2B software procurement journey will look very different from someone thinking about where to eat lunch.

So while the framework below is a good starting place, your purchase journey will likely look different than this basic template.

A note on the Support/Renew phase: It's common to see Journey Maps that include a Post-Visit Reflecting or Post-Purchase bucket.

In the example above, I've labeled this section Support/Renew, but the intention is the same.

For example, customers could still be interacting with your brand through call centers, or just reflecting on their experience of the product.

3. Touchpoints

A point of contact, interaction, or information gathering. Touchpoints can be owned by the brand (such as a TV ad or website), or reflect the brand experience in some way (such as Social Media or Amazon reviews).

Be sure to note touchpoints used during **Moments of Truth** (see point #8 below) in your Journey Map.

These Moment of Truth Touchpoints have the highest potential for impact on your customer experience.

Below you'll find a snip from our example Journey Map of the touchpoint section.

You might notice that some touchpoint sequences look linear and some are circular:

This format is to differentiate between interaction with touchpoints that is linear. For example, at a restaurant people wouldn't interact with an employee to pay before they've seen the menu.

By showing the menu and then the payment system as touchpoints in a linear journey, we understand the customer's experience a little better.

In a circular touchpoint layout, as above, we don't know when the customer will get an email versus visiting the Facebook page. In fact, emails might drive people to the Facebook page and then to the website (or vice-versa).

In this case it makes more sense to show them in a circular layout, as the process is more of a cycle than a liner interaction with touchpoints.

4. Customer Actions, Thoughts, and Verbatims

Capturing the combination of what customers do, think, and feel is why Journey Maps are so useful.

Customer verbatims (quotes) help us understand how people perceive our CX efforts and how we can improve their experience.

5. Pain Points

Here we capture the most significant hurdles, challenges or issues that customers have when trying to accomplish their mission. Each pain point will be bucketed into a part of the Purchase Journey and associated with a touchpoint (or lack thereof).

While performing qualitative research to construct your Journey Map, you'll find that customers are pretty straightforward with their complaints.

The challenge will be using data and further analysis to decide which (of likely many) of these to include.

6. Emotional Journey

This is the secret sauce that makes Customer Journey Maps especially helpful. By understanding the peaks and valleys in your customer's emotions, you'll identify those areas where your experience is outstanding, and where it could use some work.

In further writing, I explore the Peak-End Rule— a behavioral psychology principal that will make the strategy behind prioritizing repair on the very worst and final parts of your customer journey clear.

7. Opportunities for Improvement

This section is where you can build on the pain points, emotional journey, and customer feedback to start painting a picture of the future. Often these areas act as thought starters for more robust research projects or CX initiatives.

8. Moments of Truth

The moments in which your brand has the most significant opportunity to influence customer decision, opinion, or action. These typically occur when the customer first encounters your product, when they purchase your product, use it, and then react to how it works.

5 Guiding Principals for a Killer Customer Journey Map

Customer Journey Maps may vary in specific sections and design, but they all share several guiding principals:

I. **They're written from the customer's point of view, not the company's.** The purpose of the Journey Map is to close the Empathy Gap between marketer and consumer. This can be tricky to do from inside an organization. That's why I recommend brands hire an agency to build their Journey Maps, to get the benefit of an outsider's view.

2. **They combine the mechanics of an experience with the customer's emotional response.** Here's where the magic happens. The magic of Journey Maps doesn't come from just documenting a customer's experience. It comes from combining this with the intangible layer of emotions and perceptions of a customer. One without the other is a story without substance (or vice versa).

3. **They document the customer's omnichannel journey.** Journey Maps capture how people use multiple touchpoints (not just a website or retail store, for instance). From a customer's view, every interaction is part of one big experience. There's no online or offline, above-the-line or below it. It's just one company, one product, and one experience.

4. **They are visualization tools, first and foremost.** The challenge of managing the customer journey is a huge one, but the reward is equally big. To get buy-in for CX initiatives, you'll need everyone on the same page regarding pain points, challenges, and opportunities. The visual nature of the CJM has two benefits. One, everyone gets closer to understanding the complexities of your customer experience. Two, you can use it as a socialization tool to gain alignment and buy-in from internal partners.

5. **They define and capture the phases of the**

customer purchase or experience journey.
Ultimately, customer experience initiatives need to drive ROI. By aligning the Journey Map to a customer path with a measurable goal, you can keep everyone focused. Without this high-level target, it's easy to get lost in tactical initiatives that drive short-term action, but no long-term gains.

Customer Journey Map Basics: A Checklist

- Does your Customer Journey Map focus on just one persona?
- Does it follow the purchase/interaction journey across all sales channels?
- Does your Customer Journey Map include both mechanical and emotional customer measures (thoughts, feelings, pain points, emotional responses, etc.)?
- Did you include and indicate key Moments of Truth in your map?
- Does it contain opportunities for innovation, based off of the pain points and Moments of Truth you identified?

Including the elements above will ensure that your Journey Map is customer-centric, insightful, and useful to your organization. In the next section, we'll dive deeper into the Persona section of the Customer Journey Map.

∾

Key Terms

Touchpoints

Any place where customers interact with your brand. Can be service opportunities, communications, advertising, digital (website, social, etc.), customer service, retail interactions, etc.

Moments of Truth

The moments in which your brand has the greatest opportunity to influence customer decision, opinion, or action. These typically occur when the customer first encounters your product, when they purchase your product, use it, and then react to how it works.

Customer Actions, Thoughts, and Verbatims

The section that captures what customers do, think, and feel during their interaction with your brand, product, or service.

Emotional Journey

The emotional peaks and valleys in your customer's experience with your brand.

Pain Point

A customer problem that can be either real or perceived - if it's perceived then it's real to the customer.

Customer Segment

The common marketing practice of dividing a customer base into groups of individuals (segments) that are similar in specific ways relevant to marketing. This can include demographics, psychographics, motivations to buy, and spending habits.

Persona

A narrative representation of a particular group of your customers. This is fleshed out through quantitative and qualitative research about your existing (or ideal) customers. Usually includes images, demographics, thoughts/beliefs, lifestyle, goals, motivations, common behaviour, associated brands and shopping habits, and current perception of your brand.

～

Additional Resources

You can find more examples of Customer Journey Maps by visiting CXThatSings.com/Resources .

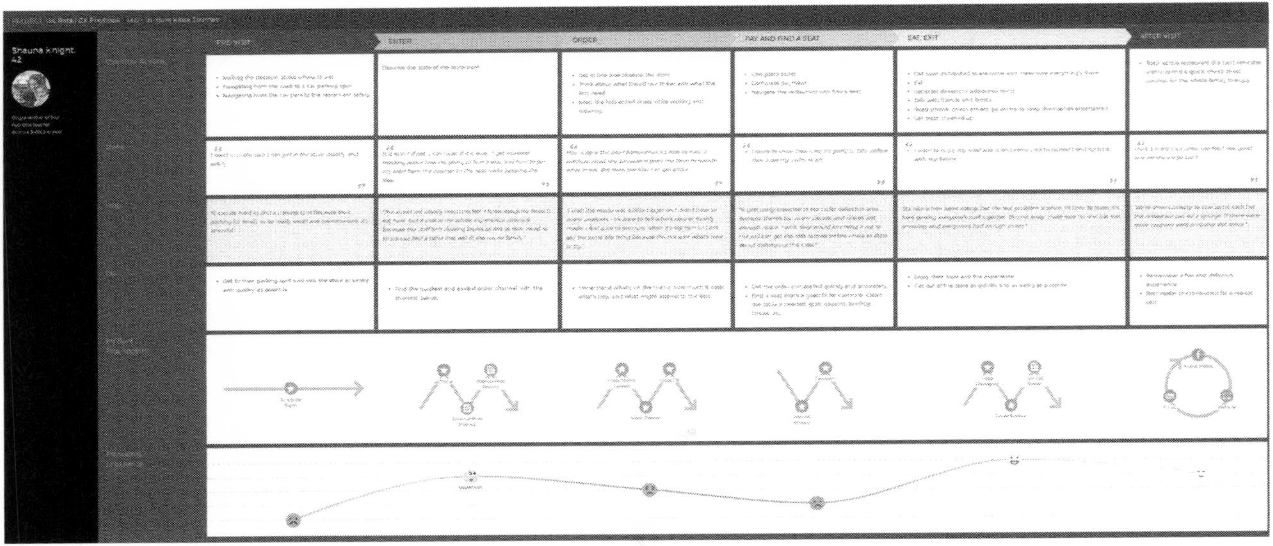
Shauna Knight, 42
ENTER
ORDER
PAY AND FIND A SEAT
EAT, EXIT
AFTER VISIT

3

MARKETING PERSONAS

YOUR JOURNEY MAP'S NORTH STAR

"Personas are often met with opposition because they're a lot of work to assemble, and once assembled they are living, evolving things and must be maintained. Like people, buyer personas change over time with the market, the times, the ebbs and flows of products and services. They absolutely require work, but they are entirely worth it."

— MarketingProfs.com

When creating your Journey Map, it's critical that you flesh out your Persona and their goals first, before heading deeper into the process. It's from this specific lens that you'll need to view your customer experience.

What is a Marketing Persona?

A marketing persona is a semi-fictional representation of a group of your customers, boiled down into one representative character. Personas bring your customers to life through both demographic and psychographic details. Based on research and data from your existing customers, a persona is a mental shortcut that represents an important segment of your buyers.

Customer focus during Persona development is crucial. You'll need to listen to what the data says about their lives, beliefs, and actions. Avoid cherry-picking to support pre-existing assumptions about your customer. Don't let confirmation bias blind you from the truth about who they really are.

Take a look at the example Persona at the end of this chapter (also featured in the Personas step in Part 2, included here for our reference).

What makes a good Persona?

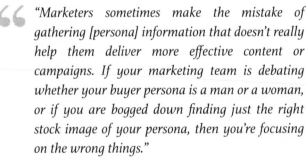

"Marketers sometimes make the mistake of gathering [persona] information that doesn't really help them deliver more effective content or campaigns. If your marketing team is debating whether your buyer persona is a man or a woman, or if you are bogged down finding just the right stock image of your persona, then you're focusing on the wrong things."
- Adele Revella, founder and president of The Buyer Persona Institute[1]

A good marketing persona makes it clear who your customer is, why they buy, and the areas of friction they face when dealing with your brand. It also gives you insight into how to talk to them in ways and places that are relevant for them.

Is there proof that we need to use Personas?

Yes, there is proof that Personas can create better results and increased ROI.

In fact, in a case study by NetProspex they found that their personas resulted in:

- 900% increase in the length of visit
- 171% increase in marketing-generated revenue
- 111% increase in email open-rate
- 100% increase in the number of pages visited

Great Marketing Personas are Based on Data

This is key. The real danger with a customer journey map is that you're not populating with data, instead you're relying on your gut to fill in the blanks. Although marketers are not generally known for empirical thinking, if you don't take the time to dig through and rely on hard data here, you'll never to get to problems at scale. This is where the "fictionalised" piece of your Persona comes in. The trick is, your Persona (let's call her Sally) may start to become an avatar for yourself or someone you know. The problem comes when you start looking to scale - data can tell you where the biggest opportunities are, and a Journey Map does need to manage to the majority in most cases (so long as that majority is in your Persona segment).

So as a point of example, if Sally is a mom who visits Target for her weekly grocery shop, and there are 100 million moms that come in to Target to do their weekly grocery shop, there's going to be some different need states that drive them in[2]. It could be that 60% of them are "value shoppers", driven in because Target has everyday low prices. 20% of them could be "status shoppers" who go to Target because it's perceived as "classier" than Wal-mart. The remaining 20% could be "health-driven shoppers" who go to Target looking for the latest health brands and organic produce. In that case, the Sally persona should take on the attributes of a "value shopper", because she makes up the majority of the "mom" segment.

3 Common Mistakes When Creating Marketing Personas

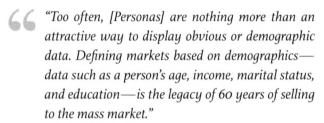

"Too often, [Personas] are nothing more than an attractive way to display obvious or demographic data. Defining markets based on demographics— data such as a person's age, income, marital status, and education—is the legacy of 60 years of selling to the mass market."

—Adele Revella, from her book "Buyer Personas: How to Gain Insight into your Customer's Expectations, Align your Marketing Strategies, and Win More Business"[3]

As with any big research project, there's a myriad of ways Journey Mapping can fall down. But there are a few common mistakes I see in the Persona portion of the exercise. We've covered these in detail in previous sections, but make sure you're avoiding the following when building your Persona.

1. **Being obvious and purely demographic.** Go

beyond the facts here. By bringing in unexpected insights and fleshing out your Persona (without getting too detailed), will help bring them to life.

2. **Focusing on your ideal customer and not your real customer.** Don't get caught up in who you think your ideal customer should be. When brands start to reject their core customer, it's often the start of a slippery trip downhill. Unless there really is a broad, organization-wide reorientation of the business happening, don't let your ego be bruised by a core Persona that may be value-focused, older, or otherwise "uncool". Not every brand can or should be hip, Millenial obsessed, Instagram-driven companies.

3. **Relying on your gut, and not allowing the data to tell a story.** I could write for hours about how marketing has become an industry that relies on "experts" far too much and "data", "education" and "research" far too little. However, for now I'll simply refer you to this Harvard Business Review[4] article that explains it far better than I could.

10 Key Questions to Answer When Developing a Marketing Persona

1. Is your core customer male, female or an even mix of both? If even, why did you choose a man or woman as your target (and does it matter)?
2. Is your persona single, married, or co-habitating?
3. Do they have kids now? If so how many and what

ages? If not, are they planning on having kids soon?

4. How old are they?
5. What's their income level?
6. How much expendable income do they have to buy your product? Do they have to make trade-offs to be able to afford it?
7. What are their 5 favorite sites, social networks, and brands?
8. If they could describe your customer experience in three words, what would those words be?
9. What kind of environment do they live in? Are they living with roommates, renting, or own their home?
10. What responsibilities and recurring costs do they have? Pets, a car, a mortgage, going out every Saturday night with friends, pedicures, etc.?

When your Persona is complete, remember to refresh it

Customer personas represent, by necessity, a snapshot in time and will evolve. Once your journey map is complete, you'll need to revisit this exercise from time to time. Given the proliferation of touchpoints, changes in the economy and your business, a yearly gut check of your persona is necessary.

Key Terms

Persona

A marketing persona is a semi-fictional representation of a group of your customers, boiled down into one representative character.

Psycographics

These are the values, fears, attitudes, aspirations, and other psychological criteria that define who your customer is, beyond the demographic facts.

Demographics

Factual information about your customer, like age, household income, location type, education, and family structure.

Name

Shauna, mother of Jackson and Harper

Personal Quote

"
I love brands that make my life easier. I need to save money and time. I don't want to waste my time trying to wade through expensive and confusing products.
"

Living situation

- Shauna recently moved back in with her retired parents after her divorce - she relies on them for childcare and emotional support. She's looking for a new place but will probably live with them for the next 12-24 months.

Demographic

🔍 Female   44   years

📍 Baltimore, Maryland

Divorced

Teacher

$45K per year

Lives with parents temporarily

Travels using a combination of public transport, Uber, and her own car.

Background

Single Mother of two
Full-time teacher
Income: $45K per year

- Shauna works full time and depends on her family for childcare. She has a masters degree in education and works 60+ hours a week to give her students the best classroom experience she can.
- She spends her small amounts of free time shopping with her mom, eating out with her kids, and occasionally splurging on an afternoon.

Motivations

- Shauna is a recently divorced mother of two young children - spending more time with them is her top priority.
- Shauna is on a tight budget - she gets child support from her ex-husband but taking care of two young kids on a teacher's salary takes its toll.
- She loves to save a buck and will trade time and convenience for value - but would prefer to get all three in one place.

Frustrations

- Shauna's torn because she wants to do well at work but with two young children at home, time and money is at a premium.
- She hates to waste money but often feels she doesn't have time to find the value button, so she relies on brands like Walmart to do the sorting for her. She'd prefer to do most of her shopping at a store with a better customer experience, like Target but "it doesn't always fit in the budget".
- She admits that Target has better prices on some things and that the Target app is really convenient. But she usually doesn't have the time to comparison shop for staples so would rather take advantage of the "Every Day Low Prices" of Walmart.

Technology

Browsers

Explorer

Channels

Favorite brand and influencers

4

THINK, DO, STOP

THE BRAIN OF YOUR CUSTOMER JOURNEY MAP

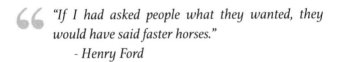

"If I had asked people what they wanted, they would have said faster horses."
  - Henry Ford

I f you're a marketer, chances are you have a picture of your brand's future— an ideal state where customers become loyal brand fans, products and services "just work," and everyone's needs are met quickly and easily.

However, when it comes to customer experience, there's always going to be a gap between where you are, and where you want to be.

You need a path to get there.

That's where the Customer Journey Map comes in.

It's from this visualization of the customer experience that you can start to collate the actions, thoughts, and feelings of your customers and develop your underlying customer experience principles.

But here's the hard truth about people: they say one thing but often do the exact opposite.

So how do you crack what customers want, when people's motivations are often a mystery to themselves?

Think of the discovery process as mining for gold. You can't just stick your shovel in the ground and start digging—you need some direction on where to start. Once you know where the gold is (customer insights) digging for it becomes much easier.

Here's 3 proven ways to get closer to your customers:

If we're trudging through a bunch of irrelevant data to discover the customer insight gold, where do we dig?

To find what your customer actually needs, you have to go beyond the superficial. Too many marketers stop with what the customer says—and not what they do and feel. The last critical piece is examining what's stopping customers from accomplishing their goals. This framework is dubbed "Do, Feel, Stop".

Too many marketers stop with what the customer says—and not what they actually do, feel, and respond to.

The "Do, Feel, Stop" Framework

The middle section of the Customer Journey Map is where you'll populate these deeper insights (don't forget there's a full page image of this map at the end of the book, and a downloadable version at CXThatSings.com/Resources):

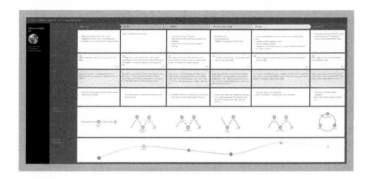

1. **What they do:** The Purchase Journey, Touchpoints, Actions
2. **What they feel:** Emotional Journey (labeled here as Customer Reaction/Feelings)
3. **What's stopping them:** Pain Points

It doesn't really matter what order these elements come in on your final map, so long as they're included.

1. What they do: The Purchase Journey

This section (also called Path to Purchase) forms the high-level framework that you'll populate with insights. It outlines the process customers follow from awareness of your brand, to purchase of your product, and beyond. In real life, this isn't a linear journey, and different sections might overlap. However, for the sake of communication, we divide the journey into discrete and step-wise parts.

Consumer brands usually have 4–6 phases in a purchase journey. In practice, you may include more, less, or different phases in your map. It all depends on your particular industry, product, and customer type. A B2B software procurement journey will look very different from someone thinking about where to eat lunch. So while the framework below is a good starting place, your purchase journey will likely look different than this basic template.

These are the general phases of a B2C consumer journey, but these will vary depending on your specific brand, sales channels, and industry.

In our example Customer Journey Map, you'll notice that our Purchase Journey is slightly different. It's divided into the following:

- Pre-Visit
- Enter
- Order
- Pay and Find a Seat
- Eat, Exit
- Post-Visit

In a retail or restaurant Customer Journey, you'll usually see something similar to the Purchase Journey above. It involves more steps inside the store, and less outside.

A note on the Support/Renew phase

t's common to see Purchase Journeys that include a Post-Visit Reflecting or Post-Purchase phase. In the example above, I've labeled this section Support/Renew, but the intention is the same. For example, customers could still be interacting with your brand through call centers, or just reflecting on their experience of the product as they use it.

Customer Touchpoints

These are all the things your customers interact with during an experience with your brand. These can be a physical or sensory interaction, a piece of communication, or human contact. They can be owned (like your website, a kiosk in your store, your app, support center, or staff) or non-owned (Googling your product, watching an unboxing video on YouTube, or reading Amazon reviews, for instance).

Document what your customers interact with on their journeys. Observe and ask. Often customers won't remember precisely what touchpoints they interacted with. I've even seen customers cite a touchpoint or interaction that never happened (hearing a "thank you" while walking out of a store, for instance).

Warning: Here's the one critical thing you can't ignore about Touchpoints

The "Customer Touchpoints" section must call-out critical

moments during the journey, called Moments of Truth. These are moments when customers are forming or change their impressions about your brand and product.

First moment of truth

When a customer is first confronted with the product, and it can happen in any owned or earned touchpoint. Procter & Gamble describe the first moment of truth as the "moment a consumer chooses a product over the other competitors' offerings," and it happens in the first few seconds a customer encounters your product or service. There's only one "first moment," so make sure it's as good an experience as possible.

Second moment of truth

This is any time the customer experiences your actual product or service, and it can happen on multiple occasions.

Third moment of truth

Not every customer gets to this moment, but for those that do, it's crucial. This is when customers feedback or react to your brand or product. Ideally, they've become brand advocates and will share their impressions with their friends and families. If they've had a terrible experience, they might still share. Just not in the way you want them to.

Customer Actions

Here's where you document the actions your customer is

taking to try and achieve their goals. How many steps do they have to take to accomplish their mission? The Emotional Journey layer (see below) will help you understand where this process may be too complicated, confusing, or even down-right infuriating for your customers.

2. What they feel: The Emotional Journey

This is what your customers feel while they're interacting with each step of your customer experience. Best tracked through biometric feedback like heartbeats per minute, eye tracking, galvanic skin response (sweat levels) and EEGs (brain monitoring), the Emotional Journey is the key to cracking your actual customer experience. Why? Because people can't filter or hide their physical response. Their body will respond when they're stressed, happy, upset or anxious. And people will remember a total experience based on select stressful moments, not every minute event.

The Emotional Journey is the key to cracking your actual customer experience because people can't hide or filter their physical response.

For example, if I call into your support line, am put on hold, and my heart rate gets faster and faster (because I'm getting angrier and angrier), it doesn't matter if you solve my problem. I'm more likely to remember the call as a poor experience because a few minutes of anger was the peak of my experience.

Why?

It's all down to a behavioral psychology phenomenon known as the Peak-End Rule.

The rule says that people remember the best or worst part (the peak) and the end of their experiences. Our brains can't remember everything about every interaction, so it takes short cuts to decide what's most important.

It's a fundamental principle in Customer Experience management, and you can learn more about it by watching Daniel Kahneman, the Nobel prize winner, explain it in his excellent TED Talk, linked here[1].

So if your customers are having a fine experience but then there's one big, consistent issue that creates an emotional response, by tracking these reactions you'll know.

3. What's stopping them: Customer Pain Points

Here's where observation, feedback, and data work hand-in-hand to create a picture of what's really bugging your customers about your experience. Capture the moments where there's a customer problem—either real or perceived. Here's where it's crucial to not just stop at the data. Have conversations, do qualitative research, and make sure you're hearing your customer's issues.

When your "Do, Think, Stop" framework is complete, use your insights to pinpoint the right opportunities for change.

Getting to the bottom of what your customers do and think is no small feat. You have to dig below the surface of what they say and look at what they do as well. Observe their behavior and ask them what they see as pain points. Then off the back of this work, consider the areas of opportunity, change, and innovation that will solve their challenges.

By digging deeply into your customers' behavior as well as their feedback, you can close the gap between where your customer experience is, and where you want it to be

Key Terms

The Purchase Journey

Also called Path to Purchase, this is outlines the process customers follow from awareness of your brand, to purchase of your product, usage, and beyond.

First moment of truth

When a customer is first confronted with the product, and it can happen in any owned or earned touchpoint.

Second moment of truth

This is is any time the customer experiences your actual product or service, and it can happen on multiple occasions.

Third moment of truth

This is when customers feedback or react to your brand or product.

Customer Actions

The actions your customer is taking to try and achieve their goals.

Customer Pain Points

The moments in your Customer Experience where there's a problem (either real or perceived), feelings of anxiety, or friction for customers.

Peak End Rule

Behavioral economics phenomenon[2] that states people remember the best or worst part (the peak) and the end of their experiences. Because our brains can't remember everything about every interaction, it takes short cuts to decide what's most important - remembering the peaks and ends of experiences helps create a story that's easier to remember.

The Emotional Journey

This is what your customers feel while they're interacting with each step of your customer experience. Best tracked through biometric feedback like heart beats per minute, eye tracking, galvanic skin response (sweat levels) and EEGs (brain monitoring), the Emotional Journey is the key to cracking your true customer experience.

Additional Resources

Videos

Daniel Kahneman, "The riddle of experience vs. memory" Ted2010 http://bit.ly/2VKtPKF

5

THE EMOTIONAL JOURNEY

THE HEART OF YOUR JOURNEY MAP

> *"Most of us think of ourselves as thinking creatures that feel, but we are actually feeling creatures that think."*
> — Jill Bolte Taylor

Toward the bottom section of our Journey Map lies the secret sauce of what makes them such valuable tools: The Emotional Journey.

The Emotional Journey is a visualization of the customer's reactions to your CX. It quantifies their emotional state and helps you quickly spot areas of friction.

A note on this template

The spectrum of human emotion is nuanced and varied. Research has shown that when asked, people use more than three words to describe their daily emotions[1]. This suggests that emotions are difficult for people to identify and report.

In this template, I've illustrated a basic look at how to measure and visualize the Emotional Journey. Depending on how nuanced you want to be with your Journey Map, you may choose a more sophisticated method of design for the Emotional Journey. However, for purposes of illustration, the Journey here is more straightforward.

The biggest customer journey mapping mistake most organizations make

There are lots of brands out there that undervalue the customer's Emotional Journey. Overlooking emotions often happens because brands underestimate how critical they are to decision-making.

But the hard truth is, emotions drive human behavior. Not rational thinking. No matter your business or industry, you're at the mercy of your customer's emotional experience with your brand.

Emotions are essential not only to how customers feel in the moment but to how they make decisions and remember experiences in the future.

It all goes back to the **Peak-End Rule**[2]. This is the behavioral psychology principle that states people remember their CX based on the peak and the end of the experience. What defines the best or worst part of the experience is how customers feel about it.

Because our brains can't remember everything about every interaction, it takes short cuts to decide what's most important. We recall the peaks and ends of experiences helps create a story that's easier to remember — the more emotional the peak or valley, the stronger the memory.

It's not how fast the customer service agent handled your issue. It's that they made you feel powerless with a lack of transparency, or if they seemed to go above and beyond to solve your problem.

No matter your customer, if you can deliver results that produce positive emotions, you will retain and acquire more customers. Because those positive emotions define how people remember your CX, you'll create an experience they'll want to repeat.

It's not just the data

Although I'm a big fan of quantitative data in marketing and consumer research, data can be deceiving in the Emotional Journey.

For instance, if you're looking at data for the car dealer Audi, it might tell a seemingly simple story. A customer researched a TT for two weeks online, got an email invite for a test drive, booked online, came into the dealer, drove the car, and then bought it. If you were only looking at data, you'd flag that as a great experience. They bought a car so the CX must be great, right? Wrong.

Let's say the salesperson saw that I was a young, single female who was in the market for a two-seater sports car, a TT. The salesperson didn't approach me for 30 minutes. When they saw me looking at TT's they suggested I try a more practical car so there'd be room for my kids. They didn't ask if I'd booked a test drive, viewed the information I'd shared online, or even asked me my name. They'd lost my booking and had to spend an hour booking me in for a new test drive. After waiting two hours outside the dealership while they detailed the car, I finally got my dream ride.

The experience made me feel unseen and ignored. It

was a good experience in the data, but a bad experience for the customer. This woman had been dreaming about buying a red TT since she was a kid. After a recent promotion, she was ready to pull the trigger on the sale. She bought the car, despite leaving furious and a little upset. It was a horrible experience. After buying her dream car, she avoided the dealership for maintenance, because thinking back on experience made her angry.

Just looking at the data would tell you that this was a successful interaction. But it wasn't. That's why it's key to measure customer emotions - the transaction data only shows you 20% of the story. Emotions fill in the remaining 80% that make or break a CX.

The hardest thing about the Emotional Journey

Capturing emotions is difficult - they're complicated and hard to measure. People experience around 5,000 different emotions that can be coded on a valence scale[3]. **Emotional Valence is the direction of a feeling, skewed in either a positive or negative direction.** It describes if the response to a stimulus makes you feel "good" or "bad." For example, roses might make someone feel happy because it reminds them of a romantic surprise from their husband. It might make others feel angry because it reminds them of the ex that cheated on them then bought roses as an apology.

For a taste of how complex tracking emotions can be, take a look at Plutchik's Wheel of Emotions below. This diagram is psychologist Robert Plutchik's attempt at classifying only a few of the 5,000 variations of emotions and how they interact.

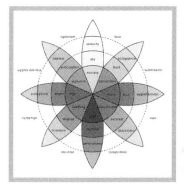

As you can see from this illustration, emotions are a complex concept. For customers, it's hard to get a deep understanding of what they're feeling. For brands, it's hard to know what customers are feeling and why it matters to the bottom line.

Because it's so difficult to get accurate self-reported feedback, we need to rely on scientific methods. Best practice is to use an autonomic research approach. Autonomic reporting tracks people's physical symptoms, things they can't easily control. Examples include galvanic skin response, EEGs, and heart rate measurements. These are more accurate[4] but can be costly and time-intensive. That makes them a harder sell for a Customer Journey project than a focus group or survey. However, their accuracy makes up for their time and financial cost.

The Emotional Journey is your Journey Map's heart. Without it, you're missing the very thing that matters most and is most overlooked, to creating a Customer Experience that sings.

Key Terms

Emotional Valence

The direction of an emotion, skewed in either a positive or negative direction. It describes if the reaction to a particular stimulus is "good" or "bad."

Valence Scale

A qualitative research method that scores emotions based on their positive or negative skew.

Autonomic Research

Research methods that measure physical feedback from customers such as heart rates, sweat on the skin (galvanic skin response), or EEG (a measure of brain activity).

Self-reported Feedback

Research methods that rely on customers to self-identify the why's and what's of an experience, then respond via a survey, focus group, or other qualitative method.

PART II

BUILDING AND USING
YOUR CUSTOMER
JOURNEY MAP

"In theory, theory and practice are the same. In practice, they are not."

    - Albert Einstein

6

INTRODUCTION TO THE PROCESS OF BUILDING A CUSTOMER JOURNEY MAP

FROM ZERO TO MAP IN FIVE EASY STEPS

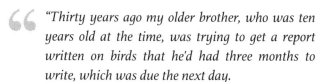

"Thirty years ago my older brother, who was ten years old at the time, was trying to get a report written on birds that he'd had three months to write, which was due the next day.

We were out at our family cabin in Bolinas, and he was at the kitchen table close to tears, surrounded by binder paper and pencils and unopened books about birds, immobilized by the hugeness of the task ahead.

Then my father sat down beside him put his arm around my brother's shoulder, and said, "Bird by bird, buddy. Just take it bird by bird."

— Anne Lamott

Now that you've had some time to understand how and why Journey Maps are created, the real fun begins.

Moving from the concept to construction of a Journey Map is no small task. Although Customer Journey Maps are incredibly useful tools, thankfully the building process isn't rocket science.

It's just a lot of hard work.

There are five basic stages when building your Map, and each stage encompasses several substages. They are:

1. Research
2. Define your Persona
3. Populate the Think, Do, Stop Model
4. Create a hypothesis map, test and design your map
5. Identify opportunities based on your research

Before diving in to each stage, let's level-set with a look at our template Journey Map from earlier in the book.

(You can also download a PDF of this template on CXThatSings.com/resources)

This template is intended to be a guide for one style of Customer Journey Map (of which there are many).

Using this template for your first or first draft of your Map is advised. Better to learn from a basic example that covers the fundamentals.

You can then build on these foundations to create your own unique bespoke spin on content, structure and design.

In the following chapters, we'll walk through each step in the process, detailing to-do's, resources, things to avoid, deliverables, expected outcomes, goals, and typical key stakeholders on the agency and client-side.

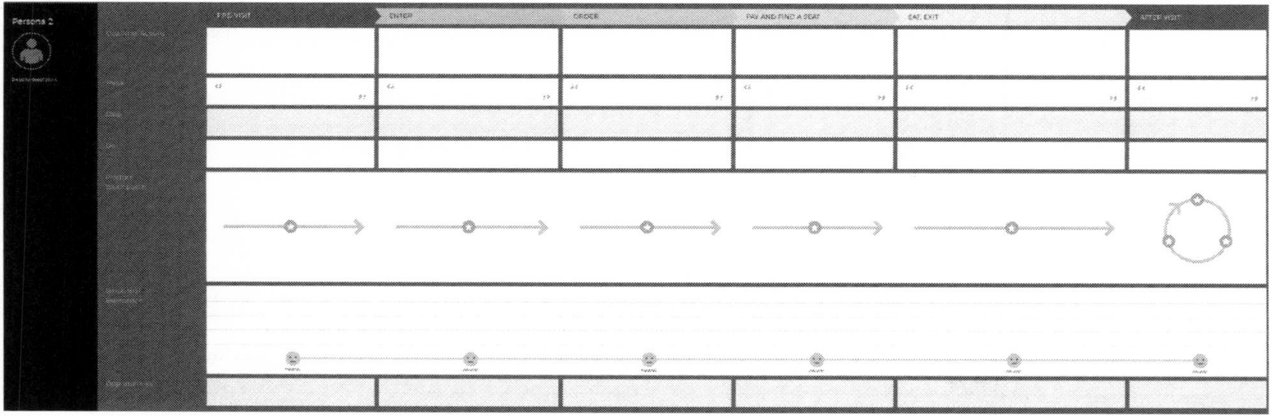
Persona 2
PRE-VISIT
ENTER
ORDER
PAY AND FIND A SEAT
EAT, EXIT
AFTER VISIT

7

STEP 1 - RESEARCH

DEFINING YOUR OBJECTIVES, UNDERSTANDING WHAT
RESEARCH EXISTING, IDENTIFYING KNOWLEDGE GAPS AND
FILLING THEM

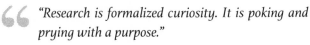 *"Research is formalized curiosity. It is poking and prying with a purpose."*
        - Zora Neale Hurston

The first stage of the Journey Map is often the hardest. In Research, you'll need to have a good understanding of what you're looking for before you go find it.

You'll have to make some hard strategic decisions about what objectives to pursue, which Personas to define, and say "no" a lot more than you say "yes".

A Note on Personas

The first stage of the research is a little "chicken and the egg", as you don't want to run off and do a ton of research that's unrelated to the Persona you choose.

But, you also don't want to lean on biased thinking and assume who your key Persona should be, before giving the data a chance to speak.

In the Research stage, stay open to the story the data is telling you. The purpose of this phase is not to find the answers. It's to define research objectives, understand what already exists, define key questions, and understand what gaps exist.

To-Do:

1. **Define your questions:** Research is only as good as the questions you ask. As the saying goes, "Ask better questions to get better answers."

2. **Discover:** Find what existing research exists around your customer, their thoughts, feelings, preferences, and how they interact with your touchpoints. Although it may not all be pertinent, you'll often find that inside big organizations, there's lots of historic data that you can leverage.

3. **Identify gaps:** Based around the questions you defined in step one, and the historic research you dug up in step two, you should be able to identify where you need to do additional research to fill in the gaps.

4. **Perform additional research:** Once your knowledge gaps are identified, you're able to start the process of observation, quantitative analysis, and quantitative research to fill in those gaps.

Resources:

Where to find data

Here's a list of common sources to find existing data for your Journey Map:

Involve the broader team

A key mistake in research is limiting key team members to marketing. Make sure to include sales, analysts, finance, IT operations, and even front-line and support staff in your research. Anyone who interacts with your customer or their data is key when exploring the customer experience.

Social media, product reviews, and call center logs

This is where your customers give you straightforward opinions about your brand. If there's something you're failing on or common roadblocks, they'll become obvious through customer support channels.

Marketing research

Existing research is invaluable. But it's not the only source for data. In fact, you're better off combining several data and research sources to avoid cherry-picking or confirmation bias. This is where quantitative data is key. If you notice something in qualitative, see if it's supported at scale. If it's a one-off comment from a focus group participant that's not found in the data, it may not be applicable to your final Journey Map.

Online customer journeys

Analysis tools like Google Analytics and Adobe are great starting places if one of your key channels is online. This isn't always the case, as some industries may have digital touchpoints that aren't often used by customers in their "most likely" journey.

But, depending on how robust your data is, you'll find this is a key resource for other brands and sites your customer frequents. Brands without digital touchpoints aren't common.

Usage and relevance of these digital touchpoints can vary, but most brands will need to consider an online component in their Journey Map.

Customer interviews, focus groups, and surveys

Who knows your customers better than they know themselves? First-person research is a critical data source. In particular, interviews can help you test your Persona hypotheses about their goals, values, needs, and pain points.

Guiding Questions

Although you'll have your own research questions specific to your organization or client, I've included a few common Guiding Questions below to get you started.

We'll create the Persona, Path to Purchase, and Think/Do/Stop sections later, but for now these questions will help you understand what to look for.

Persona:

1. Is your core customer male, female or an even mix of both? If even, why did you choose a man or woman as your target (and does it matter)?
2. Is your persona single, married, or co-habitating?
3. Do they have kids now? If so how many and what ages? If not, are they planning on having kids soon?
4. How old are they?
5. What's their income level?
6. How much expendable income do they have to buy your product? Do they have to make trade-offs to be able to afford it?
7. What are their 5 favorite sites, social networks, and brands?
8. If they could describe your customer experience in three words, what would those words be?
9. What kind of environment do they live in? Are they living with roommates, renting, or own their home?
10. What responsibilities and recurring costs do they have? Pets, a car, a mortgage, going out every Saturday night with friends, pedicures, etc.?

Path to Purchase:

- What are all the ways a specific customer interacts with your brand, product, or service?
- Have you looked at non-owned channels, such as

retailers that stock your products, Amazon reviews, and Google results?

- Have you asked your customers as well as looked at the touchpoint data? Are they saying one thing but doing another?
- Are your answers based on assumptions, or on research and data?
- Have you included qualitative as well as quantitative data in your research?
- Are you treating all your findings as hypotheses, and trying to prove them wrong (instead of right)?

Think, Do, Stop:

- Are you stopping at what customers say, or digging into what they are actually doing?
- Have you identified those key Moments of Truth where your customer is forming their most impactful opinions around your product?
- Are your answers based on assumptions, or on research and data?
- Have you dug into the places where your customers go for reviews, feedback, unboxing, or product previews?
- If your customers are saying one thing and doing another, can you identify why?
- Are you treating all your findings as hypotheses, and trying to prove them wrong (instead of right)?
- Are you a victim of confirmation bias? In other words, are you just seeing the data that confirms

what you already believe to be true or are you letting the data tell the story?

- Have there been any big changes in your customer experience (such as the introduction of new sales channels) that may be impacting your customer's actions?
- Do you have a good understanding of the customer pain points that exist? Do your customers agree or disagree with what the data is saying?
- Have you included qualitative as well as quantitative data in your research?

Deliverables:

1. **List of key research questions and objectives**
2. **Research inventory** that helps you understand what available research already exists and what it tells you. This should also fill any knowledge gaps between what you want to know and what you need to know.
3. **Additional research plan** for filing those knowledge gaps.

Key Stakeholders:

Defining and analyzing your key stakeholders is very important as you look to get cooperation from other groups in the organization. This will be different for every engagement, but the following are a good place to start:

- Marketing
- IT
- Digital, UX/UI Designers
- Usability Testing and Design
- Product Management/Design
- Brand Management
- Customer Support and Call Centers
- Retail Employees and Management
- Customer Experience groups inside the company
- External research vendors and consultancies
- Operations
- Legal
- Agency strategists and accounts/client services
- Leadership across the organization

Once you identify who your key stakeholders are and what they need, the next step is to analyze them. Categorize the people you'll work with during this project on the following axes:

HIGH INFLUENCE LOW INTEREST *"Latents"*	HIGH INFLUENCE HIGH INTEREST *"Promoters"*
LOW INFLUENCE LOW INTEREST *"Apathetics"*	LOW INFLUENCE HIGH INTEREST *"Defenders"*

1. **Latents:** These are the people who are high up in

the organization but don't really care about the project itself. They may know it's happening, but it's not on their day-to-day radar. These people won't need to be contacted much, except maybe a cursory email from the client project lead, sharing the final product. It's unlikely that you'll interact with these people much.

2. **Apathetics:** These are the people who have little power and no interest in what you're doing. There's no need to update these stakeholders or keep them in the loop as they don't care what you're up to, and they have no power with which to help or hinder you.

3. **Defenders:** These are the people you're more likely to work with on a day-to-day basis. They're likely Project, Marketing, or other general business Managers (depending on the title structure of the company) or below. They might be a little junior, but they are very invested in the outcome of your project. You'll communicate with this group this most, as you're likely to work with them the most as well. Keep them in the loop, they're your army of allies inside the company.

4. **Promoters:** These people are your calvary. They have significant clout in the company, so they're able to pick up the phone to help you get over a sticky roadblock during the project. But don't call them for every little favor. They'll get key updates during the project, and will need to be sold into your final Journey Map, so keep them in the loop and make sure they feel heard. The final product will live or die on their say-so.

8

STEP 2 - DEFINE YOUR PERSONA

YOU HAVE TO UNDERSTAND WHO YOUR CUSTOMER IS,
BEFORE YOU CAN LEARN WHAT THEY NEED.

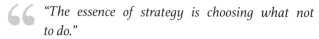 *"The essence of strategy is choosing what not to do."*
　　　　- Michael Porter

The marketing persona you define will set the stage for thousands of decisions that come after. It will determine who you communicate with, how to speak to them, when to message them, and how to tailor the customer experience to their needs.

By taking the time to flesh out the Persona, you'll ensure that you're designing future state for exactly what this customer needs.

～

To Do:

- Decide which customer segment is the right one to blow out into a full-fledged Persona

- Develop your customer Persona by understanding their lives, needs, demographics, and psychographics.

∾

Guiding Questions

1. Is your core customer male, female or an even mix of both? If either, why did you choose a man or woman as your target (and does it matter)?
2. Is your persona single, married, or co-habitating?
3. Do they have kids now? If so how many and what ages? If not, are they planning on having kids soon?
4. How old are they?
5. What's their income level?
6. How much expendable income do they have to buy your product? Do they have to make trade-offs to be able to afford it?
7. What are their 5 favorite sites, social networks, and brands?
8. If they could describe your customer experience in three words, what would those words be?
9. What kind of environment do they live in? Are they living with roommates, renting, or own their home?
10. What responsibilities and recurring costs do they have? Pets, a car, a mortgage, going out every Saturday night with friends, pedicures, etc.?

∾

Key Elements of a Marketing Persona

When developing a marketing persona, it can be tempting to include every detail under the sun. However, there are a few fundamental attributes all personas should include:

Photo

A photo that represents your persona is a key visual tool. It can be tempting to grab the first stock photo you find that's a general match for your core customer, but that's not ideal. A better representation is a real-life picture from first-person research. It's more relatable, and it'll help you step out of the echo chamber that too many businesses find themselves in.

Name

It's a simple as "Jill" or "The Haverford Family". Naming your persona is a small detail that will bring them to life. It'll also make it easier to reference your customer when discussing their journey.

Demographics

Factual information about your customer, like age, household income, location type, education, and family structure are all essential details. They help you empathize with your persona's day-to-day life and struggles.

It's important to remember that your customer isn't spending all day thinking about your brand. Therefore, don't treat them like they come to life the moment they step through your doors.

Psychographics

These are the values, fears, attitudes, aspirations, and other psychological criteria that define who your customer is, beyond the facts. These can include:

- Hobbies
- Levels of mobile adoption and computer literacy
- Where they get their news
- Other brands they love
- Where they go to get updates about their friends, family, and the world around them.

Psychographics help you answer the question, "Why do they buy?".

The persona is part real and part fictionalized, but make sure you're still relying on data from real customers to create it.

Limit your Journey Map to the experience of one persona and their path toward one primary goal. Because the primary goal of a CJM is to bring clarity to an ambiguous buying process, if you try to capture every customer and every journey in one map, you'll miss the signal in the noise.

The persona below is the same example we worked through in the early chapter on personas.

If you want to take a look at more example personas, I've included them in the third section, "Examples, References, and Bonus Information".

Please note, the brands featured are used as points of example. They in no way represent an endorsement by or involvement by these brands with this persona, "CX That Sings", or the author.

Deliverables:

- **Persona document**

Goals:

The persona is your first concrete step in creating your Journey Map. After your persona is defined, you'll be able to pull supporting research to see what information exists about them already.

Keep their photo and key information up on the wall of your project room. Continue to stress-test future insights and conclusions against their world, not yours.

This persona will be your North Star for the remainder of the Customer Journey Map project.

Key Stakeholders:

- Project team and team managers
- Client sponsor (day-to-day)
- Marketing
- UI/UX Researchers
- Consumer Researchers
- Strategists
- Accounts/Client Services

Digital Resource Reminder: Example Personas

The Persona on the next page can also be found in digital form on CXThatSings.com/Resources if you'd like to take a more detailed look at the image.

Name

Shauna, mother of Jackson and Harper

Personal Quote

" I love brands that make my life easier. I need to save money and time. I don't want to waste my time trying to wade through expensive and confusing products. "

Living situation

- Shauna recently moved back in with her retired parents after her divorce - she relies on them for childcare and emotional support. She's looking for a new place but will probably live with them for the next 12-24 months.

Background

Single Mother of two
Full-time teacher
Income $45K per year

- Shauna works full time and depends on her family for childcare. She has a masters degree in education and works 90+ hours a week to give her students the best classroom experience she can.
- She spends her small amounts of free time shopping with her mom, eating out with her kids, and occasionally splurging on an afternoon.

Demographic

 Female   years
 Baltimore Maryland

Divorced

Teacher

34-51 per year

Lives with parents temporarily

Travels using a combination of public transport (bus) and her car.

Technology

Browsers

 Explorer

Channels

Motivations

- Shauna is a recently divorced mother of two young children - spending more time with them is her top priority.
- Shauna is on a tight budget - she gets child support from her ex-husband but taking care of two young kids on a teacher's salary takes its toll.
- She loves to save a buck and will trade time and convenience for value - but would prefer to get all three in one place.

Frustrations

- Shauna's torn because she wants to do well at work but with two young children at home, time and money is at a premium.
- She hates to waste money but often feels she doesn't have time to find the value notion, so she relies on brands like Walmart to do the sorting for her. She'd prefer to do most of her shopping at a store with a better customer experience, like Target but "it doesn't always fit in the budget".
- She admits that Target has better prices on some things and that the Target app is really convenient. But she usually doesn't have the time to comparison shop for staples so would rather take advantage of the "Every Day Low Prices" of Walmart.

Favorite brand and influencers

9

STEP 3 - POPULATE THE THINK, DO, STOP MODEL

"Your most unhappy customers are your greatest source of learning."
   -Bill Gates

The Think, Do, Stop model is the brain of your Customer Journey map. It records what's happening, without assumption or bias. Be honest in this section and use it to tell some uncomfortable truths (or surprising good news) to your clients and colleagues.

Although it may seem straightforward, you'll find this is the phase where biased thinking will start to raise its ugly head. Don't go with your gut here. Make sure to lean on the data to tell the story, and check for Confirmation Bias throughout the process.

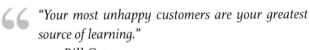

To Do:

Record your research

Start collating your findings and insights from the Research phase.

I recommend writing the exciting bits from your research down on sticky notes, but digital platforms like Evernote can work too. But in general, it's more helpful to have these insights at hand in a visual way so you can interact with them, move them around quickly, and see everything in one place.

Organize your research

Find a big whiteboard or wall. Draw or print out the common phases to a Purchase Journey (also called Path to Purchase).

Then, start grouping your sticky notes under the correct phase of the customer journey. As you put them up, look for patterns and common threads.

Whenever you see something interesting, make a note or create a sub-group.

Design your Purchase Journey / Path to Purchase

You may find that all your notes fit under the established phases perfectly. But more often than not, you'll notice that your brand has specific stages that don't quite fit in this general template. That's totally fine!

This template is a general guide to help structure research and findings - commonly, the language and specific phases of this illustration need to be tweaked.

Let the customer insights guide you. You don't need to force your journey map into these phases if they aren't a perfect fit.

Populate your Path to Purchase

Now that you've completed the Path to Purchase framework, start dividing your sticky notes into Think, Do, and Stop categories. You may find it easier to populate "Do" first, as this will make organizing your customer verbatim and thoughts easier.

Think: These can include customer quotes from qualitative research, sentiment analysis from social media, and other verbatim. It's anything your customer has expressed or an opinion they hold about any part of the customer journey.

Do: This section includes Touchpoints, Moments of Truth, and customer actions they take to achieve a goal. Any action the customer takes belongs in this section.

Stop: Here is where you'll fill in moments where your customers experience pain points or issues. These challenges will come through via customer verbatim, process bottlenecks, cart abandonment and dropoff data, or anything else that indicates the experience has been interrupted.

∽

Guiding Questions

Although your questions will vary depending on your customer, industry, and products, below are a few thought-starter questions to get you thinking in the right way.

What they think

1. What are customers saying about your journey? Are there obvious things they love and/or hate?
2. How are they reacting in general - do they love or hate your brand?
3. When customers complain, what are the areas they're complaining the most about? Can you stack rank these via data or use Wordclouds on their verbatims to better understand what issues are jumping to the fore?
4. Why do they choose your brand or certain products? Who are you competing with?
5. How do they consider your brand before they enter a store or visit your website/app?
6. What customer needs or ocasions bring them to your brand?

What they do:

1. What owned touchpoints do customers interact with? What non-owned touchpoints? How are they using each of these?
2. Where are the Moments of Truth, where your

customer is interacting with your product for the first time?

3. Where are they going to spread the good news about your brand? Are they talking about their car on Facebook? Sharing pictures of the amazing meal they just ate? Make sure you know where they're sharing bad news as well.

4. Where are they going to get feedback about your brand? Product reviews? YouTube? Make sure you're considering the non-owned channels that are driving significant traffic to your site.

What's stopping them:

1. What parts off the experience do your customers hate? What's causing them discomfort, anger, sadness, or just plain boredom?

2. Where are the bottlenecks in your experience? Places where the CX slows down, where lots of thinking or effort is required from a customer?

3. Is there any touchpoint that's difficult to navigate? Does your data show a significant drop-off or abandoned cart rate during any part of the experience?

~

Deliverables:

- You should move on from this section only after you've had enough time to consider the existing

data and new research in the context of
Think/Do/Stop.

- The Path to Purchase should be built in this
  section
- The Hypothesis Customer Journey should be
  build (minus the Emotional Journey) in
  this phase

∼

Key Stakeholders:

For this section of the process, key stakeholders will likely
be limited to the core members of the Customer Journey
Map team and their project sponsor.

10

STEP 4 - CREATE A HYPOTHESIS MAP, TEST, AND DESIGN YOUR MAP

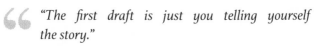

"The first draft is just you telling yourself the story."
— Terry Pratchett

This phase of construction is about bringing all the information together, condensing it, cleaning it up, and putting it into a design format for testing.

To Do:

- Layer Emotional Journey data onto the existing Think/Do/Stop and Purchase Journey sections of the Map
- Hypothesis Map Development Session
- Create complete Hypothesis Customer Journey Map
- Hypothesis Map testing sessions with real customers

- Amend and shape your final Customer Journey Map
- Design and circulate your Customer Journey Map

Objectives:

In the Test phase, you'll be asking the following questions:

1. Did we accurately capture all the phases and steps that customers go through from awareness/need state to purchase and renewal?
2. Did we really discover all the customer pain points?
3. Do our customer thoughts/emotions/verbatims resonate with what real customers in our persona think and feel?
4. Did we accurately identify leakage points?

Resources:

Common Tactics for Testing with Customers

There are many different ways you can validate a map with real customers. But no matter how you perform this research, be sure to pull participants from your target Persona, or most of their input will be invalid.

In general, you will find that this step involves qualitative, not quantitative research. Talking to real customers in these personas tends to produce the most valuable insight.

Three of the most common tactics to validate a Hypothesis Map include:

- Focus groups
- One-on-one Interviews
- Surveys

I'd recommend 5-8 sessions if possible, with three as a bare minimum to achieve reliable and repeatable results.

Basically, you're trying to do two things:

1. Get feedback on what you have
2. Get more insight on what their ideal experience would be

Running these sessions is time-consuming (usually 3-4 hours long) and you should be sure not to lead the customers to get sucked into that confirmation bias we talked about earlier.

Testing thought-starters

1. Have these customers map the journey before seeing the Hypothesis Map (this is best described to customers as "tell me the story..." or "draw your experience..." of achieving a certain goal). Prompt them on the touchpoints they remember using, how helpful they found them.

What did they like or dislike about their experience.

2. Show customers the Hypothesis Map, walk them through it, and react to it.
3. Have them describe their "ideal experience" - in a perfect world how would this customers achieve their goal? What would change?

Example Customer Journey Maps:

CXthatsings.com/resources

≈

Deliverables:

- Sketched Hypothesis Map
- Test findings from a focus group, interviews, or surveys
- Beautifully designed Customer Journey Map ready to share

≈

Expected Outcomes:

In a perfect world, every survey, focus group, and interview will reconfirm your findings. But, more than likely, some rework will have to be done.

By designing a hypothesis map and stress testing it with real customers, you'll ensure that Confirmation Bias hasn't kicked in during the construction.

If there's an element that doesn't ring true with customers, you'll find out.

Once you have your findings from a focus group or interviews, you'll move on to the last step, designing your Customer Journey Map in a beautiful and shareable way.

Key Stakeholders:

- Project team and team managers
- Client sponsor (day-to-day)
- Client sponsor (leadership)
- Designers and Art Directors
- UI/UX Researchers
- Consumer Researchers
- Strategists
- Accounts/Client Services

11

STEP 5 - IDENTIFY OPPORTUNITIES BASED ON YOUR RESEARCH

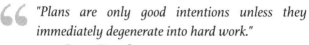 *"Plans are only good intentions unless they immediately degenerate into hard work."*
- Peter Drucker

Now that you have a finished customer journey map, the fun begins. The final layer to add is the "Opportunities" area, where you get to propose solutions that overcome your customers' pain points.

To Do:

- Hold an opportunity brainstorming session to identify next steps for CX improvement.

Best Practice for Opportunity Brainstorm Sessions

The future of your customer experience improvement projects will stem from this brainstorming session. These must be run with the end-goal of developing a project plan.

1. Structure your session around questions related to key pain points.

Research shows that loose and free brainstorming sessions are less productive than approaches with more structure.[1]

According to research by McKinsey[2], these key questions should have two characteristics:

- Questions that force participants to take a new and unfamiliar perspective.
- Questions that limit the scope your team will explore. *However, make sure these questions aren't so restrictive that they box participants into limited outcomes.*

2. Make sure the right people are in the room

Make sure these brainstorming participants represent not only their departments but the right level within those departments.

Given the strategic importance of developing a Journey Map, these are generally more senior people. But if they're too high in the organization, they might be disconnected from the real pain points of customers.

Strike a balance between seniority and connection with the day-to-day.

3. Include 2-3 "fearless foreigners" in your group

It's best to include a few people who have no direct experience with the project. You want people whose working style, worldview, and skills are wildly different from the core team.

These people are more likely to ask "why" and off-the-wall questions since they don't know they aren't supposed to.

~

Expected Outcomes:

Off the back of your brainstorming session(s), you can begin to prioritize the opportunities. After understanding what low-hanging fruit projects exist, you can start to build a long-term plan.

~

Key Stakeholders:

- Marketing
- IT
- Digital, UX/UI Designers
- Usability Testing and Design
- Product Management/Design
- Brand Management
- Customer Support and call centers
- Retail Employees and Management
- Customer Experience groups inside the company
- External research vendors and consultancies
- Operations
- Legal
- Agency strategists and accounts/client services
- Leadership across the organization

PART III

EXAMPLES, REFERENCES, AND BONUS INFORMATION

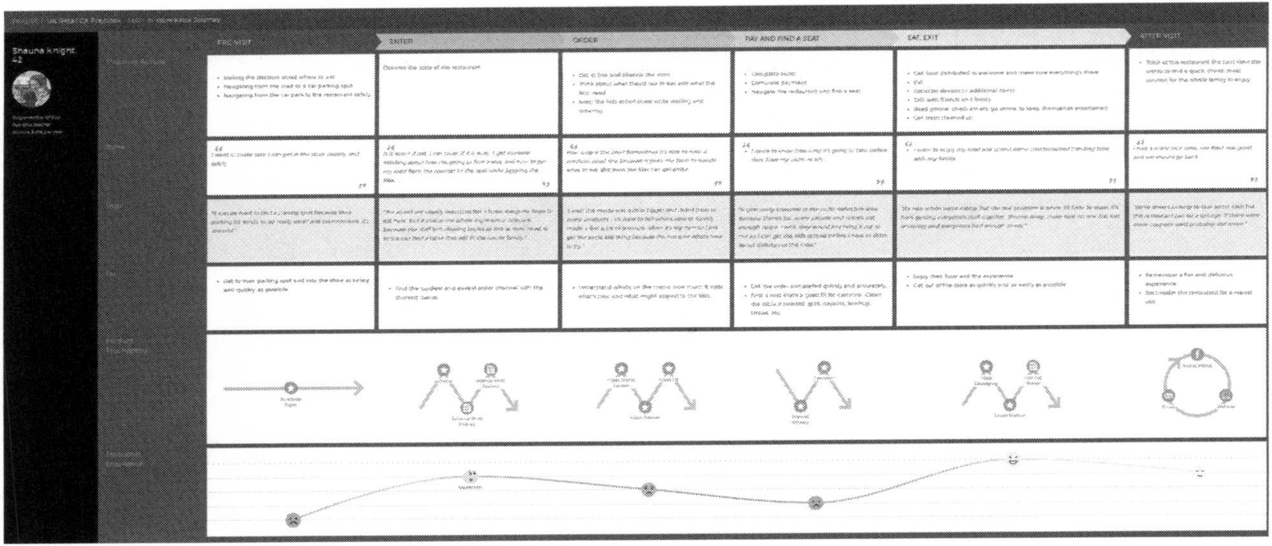

Shauna Knight
42
ENTER
ORDER
PAY AND FIND A SEAT
EAT, EXIT
AFTER VISIT

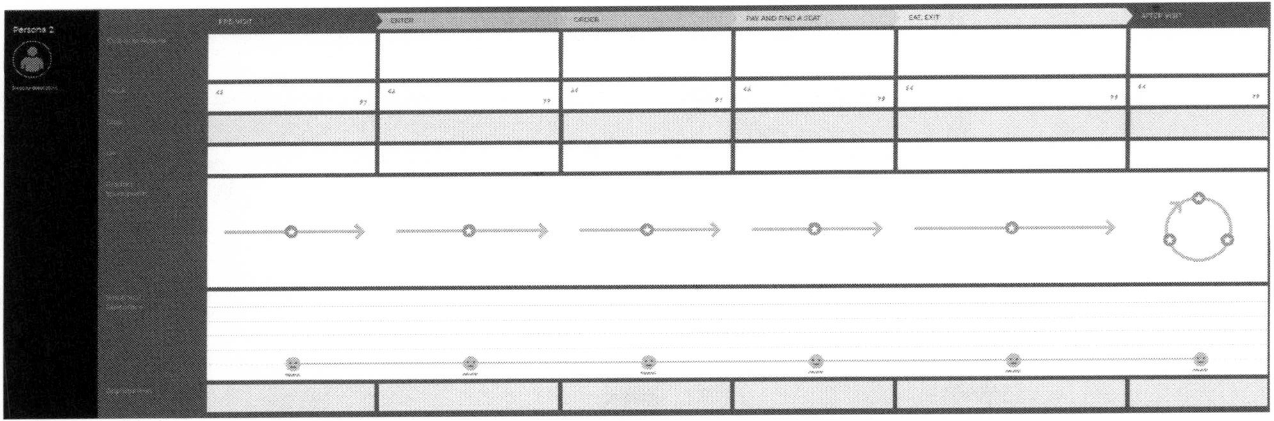
Persona 2
PRE-VISIT
ENTER
ORDER
PAY AND FIND A SEAT
EAT, EXIT
AFTER VISIT

12

JOURNEY MAP EXAMPLE #1: FAST FOOD DRIVE THRU JOURNEY

I n this example, we're looking at a family considering Fast Food destinations.

Their consideration period is likely short, as they only seek out the experience when their need state (hunger or need for a pick-me-up) strikes.

The lens through which we're creating this journey is a dad with one child (The Palmer Family). He's stopped in because the kid is getting fussy, there are no snacks in the car, and Dad could use some caffeine after a long day out.

The journey is detailed on the next page, but as always is also available for download at CXThatSings.com/Resources.

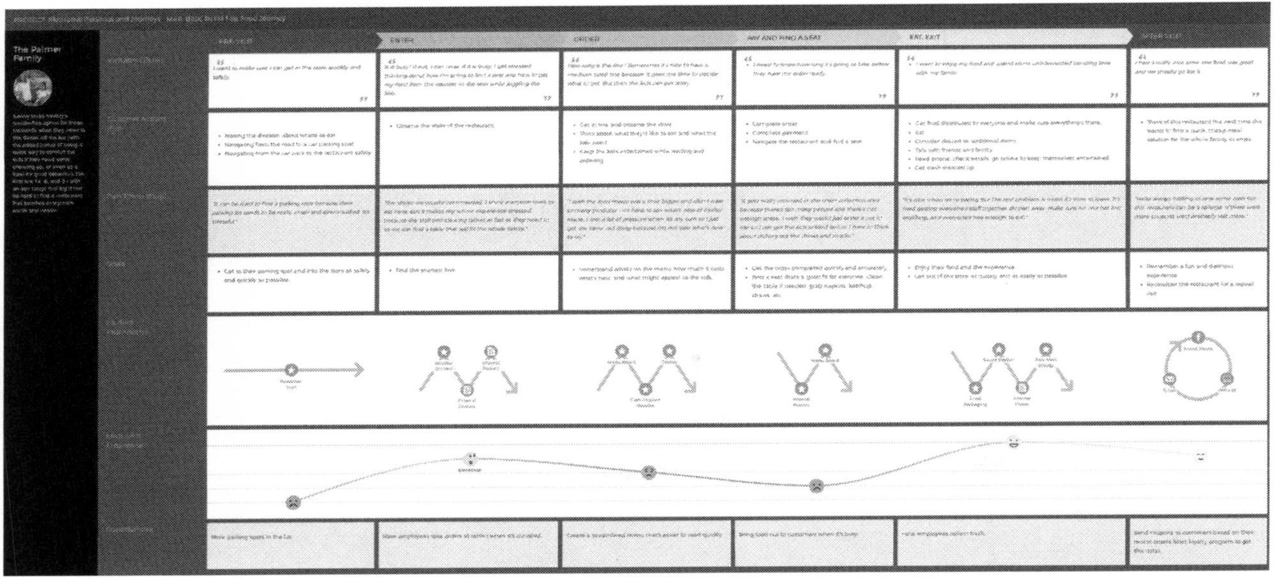
The Palmer Family
ENTER
ORDER
EAT, EXIT

13

JOURNEY MAP EXAMPLE #2: RAIL TICKETS BOOKING JOURNEY

I n this example, we're exploring a U.S. customer (Katie Voase) who is trying to book rail tickets, while still in the States, for a vacation in Japan.

Their consideration period is a medium length, as they are trying to plan the rest of their vacation around available rail tickets and times.

The lens through which we're creating this journey is a single woman who is traveling alone. This is a dream destination for Katie, but she's traveling on a budget, and has never been abroad.

The journey is detailed on the next page, but as always is also available for download at CXThatSings.com/Resources.

Katie Voase

14

JOURNEY MAP EXAMPLE #3: ECOMMERCE SITE - ATHLETIC FOOTWEAR JOURNEY

I n this example, we're looking at our Sam Carter persona who is in the market for some new athletic shoes.

The consideration period for this product is a little longer than our previous examples, because there's no time constraints on when he needs to buy. However, his budget does provide some challenges.

The lens through which we're viewing this journey is Sam, a man who is looking for something fashionable but also cares about his environmental impact.

The journey is detailed on the next page, but as always is also available for download at CXThatSings.com/Resources.

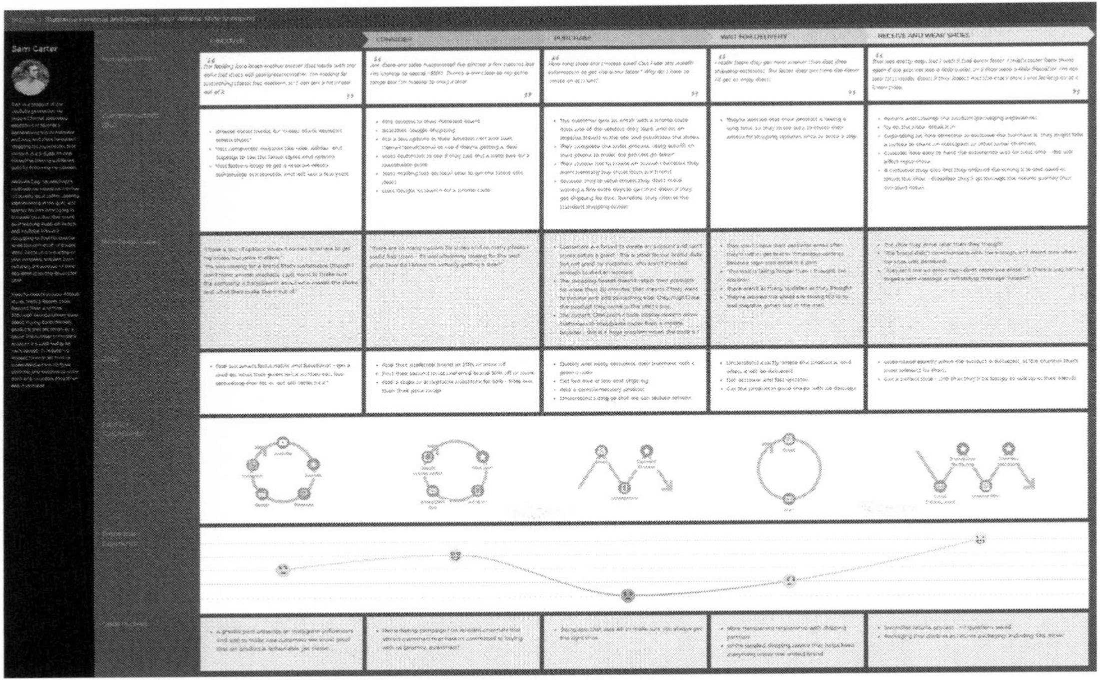
Sam Carter
CONSIDER
PURCHASE
WAIT FOR DELIVERY
RECEIVE AND WEAR SHOES

15

PERSONA EXAMPLE #1: THE PALMER FAMILY

This example persona was used to create the Fast Food example journey featured earlier in this section.

The Palmer Family is headed up by Kenny and includes his children. Kenny is the "decider" in the family, but his kids also influence when and where he decides to buy. Some of their favorite brands include Chick-fil-a, Panera, Disney, Walmart, Nintendo Switch, and YouTube.

When Kenny is with the kids during the week, it's because he's chauffeuring them from one activity to another, or back home after school. Therefore, they prize brands that are fun, fast, and dependable - Kenny's got enough on his plate without a fussy kid.

The persona is detailed on the next page, but as always is also available for download at CXThatSings.com/Resources.

The Palmer Family (Kenny Palmer, Dad/Shopper)

♂ Male   44   years

📍 Atlanta Georgia

Married

Manager - Corporate

$85k

Channels

Technology

Goals

· Needs something quick and easy (and it means they don't have to get out of the car to handle the kids or take time to cook when they do get home)

Quote

❝ I take the kids to a fast food place when we need a break and they've been well-behaved. It's a reward for everybody. ❞

Background

Kenny loves having a hassle-free option for those moments when they need to tick dinner off the list (with the added bonus of being a quick way to comfort the kids if they need some cheering up, or even as a treat for good behavior). His kids are 14, 6, and 3 - with an age range that big it can be hard to find a restaurant that satisfies everyone's wants and needs.

Motivations

- Grabbing a quick meal to treat the kids for behaving during the school run and after school activities
- They'll eat most of their fries in the car, but what's left over they'll enjoy on the couch in front of the TV
- Dad wants a little treat for himself as well, but he's not as familiar with the menu as his kids (who have more time to read the menu)

Frustrations

- The line is always long in the drive thru, but it can take a short time. He's never sure which way to go - in the store or outside of it.
- His food sometimes isn't right, and that means the kids will get upset.
- There's a lot of time pressure in the line, which makes him stressed.

16

PERSONA EXAMPLE #2: KATIE VOASE

O ur next persona was used to create the "Rail Ticket" customer journey. If you haven't checked it out, it's Journey Map Example #2 in Part III.

Katie is 28, value-driven, but also aspirational. She lives for her Instagram likes but still needs to party on a budget.

Her favorite brands are a mix of achievable and aspirational - such as Whole Foods, Target, Yves Saint Laurent, and Everlane. Her wardrobe is a mix of these "high" and "low" brands, but her expectation for each brand experience is to being treated like she's unique and special.

Katie likes brands that know her preferences, suggest things she might like, and personalizes her experience as much as possible. That way, she gets the feeling of a custom, VIP experience that always caters for her jam-packed lifestyle (and lack of time).

∿

The persona is detailed on the next page, but as always is also available for download at CXThatSings.com/Resources.

Goals

Katie's always on the lookout for a new adventure but she also needs to snag a deal, and she's willing to work a little harder to find one.

Quote

"
I'm always on the lookout for an exciting new place to travel that's different than the "trendy" places. Money is a concern, so I can't always jet set off to exactly where I'd like, but I am able to take extended vacations so that helps me pack more in for less.
"

Katie Voase

 Female   28   years

 Richmond, Virginia

Single

Teacher

$45k

Background

- Katie has two passions in life - travel and her career. In fact, a large part of her decision to become a teacher was so she could spend her summers seeing the world.
- Travel and planning for travel are Katie's favorite hobbies. However, she isn't able to plan as early in advance as she'd like, because her budget forces her to take advantage of last-minute deals much of the time.

Technology

Motivations

- Katie loves the feeling of being free, so she loves brands and products that make it easy to pick up and leave, pause, or cancel their service easily.
- Katie loves sharing her travels with family and friends. The more interesting her adventures, the better - there's a lot of people living vicariously through her online!
- Risk is something that Katie loves but in small doses. While she won't be climbing Mt. Everest any time soon, she does love to go off the beaten path when she can.

Frustrations

- Between work, keeping fit, online courses, and her side gig Katie doesn't have a lot of time to go shopping. She needs brands that come to her, and relies on subscription services to taste-make.
- Although Katie has been teaching for a while, her income never seems to keep up with her taste for travel. She's always on the lookout for last minute deals, friends to travel with, or ways to make her dollar go farther overseas.
- Airline tickets are Katie's biggest expense, so the longer she can make her total trip, the better. That way she only has to fly international once, but can then see lots of local spots without spending too much more.

Channels

17

PERSONA EXAMPLE #3: SAM CARTER

T he last bonus persona example, Sam Carter, was used to create the Athletic Shoe eCommerce customer journey.

When it comes to customers, Sam's pretty needy. He asks a lot from the brands he buys, and even though money's tight, he's willing to splurge a little on products that pass his tests. Like many people of his generation, Sam is environmentally conscious and wants to know where his brands source their products.

Sam's favorite companies are transparent, responsible, but also stylish - Allbirds shoes, Harry's Razors, Levis, Beyond Meat, and Nike. Sam wants the products he chooses to say something positive about him.

The persona is detailed on the next page, but as always is also available for download at CXThatSings.com/Resources.

NAME

Sam Carter

PERCENTAGE OF OUR CUSTOMER BASE

 55 %

TYPE

Artisan

Quote

" I like brands that help me express myself and my brand. I'm looking for sustainable, but trendy products that really help me express me.   *"*

Background

Sam is a product of the YouTube generation. He skipped formal secondary education in favor of a backpacking trip to Australia and Asia, and there he started vlogging his experiences. Not content in a 9-5 job, he sees himself as blazing a different path by following his passion.

He loves Gary Vaynerchuck's motivational videos you thrives on quality local coffee, recently started lifting in the gym, and spends his free time trying to increase his subscriber count by streaming PubG on Twitch and YouTube. He's still struggling to find his creative voice but isn't short of a work ethic. Sam's vlog is starting to pick up speed and he's been reducing the amount of time he's been spending driving for Uber.

Favorite brands include Allbirds shoes, Harry's Razors, Levis, Beyond Meat, and Nike. Although Sam genuinely cares about buying Earth-friendly products that are driven by a cause, the number in his bank account is a stark reality he can't escape. To reduce his impact, he recycles, tries to understand where his food, clothing, and electronics come from and considers himself an eco-minimalist.

Demographic

 Male   21   years

 Austin, Texas

Single

Self-employed Content Creator and Uber Driver

$26k per year

Technology

Channels

Motivations

- Following his passion
- Expressing his point of view
- Recognition in the form of likes and followers
- Following his own rules, schedule and path
- Traveling with friends, especially to "Instagrammable" locations
- Understanding his environmental impact on the world around him and reducing it
- Connecting with others in his community to share ideas, stories, and skills

Frustrations

- Sam finds it hard to spend so much time on his own, with no clear path and few connections in his life that have found success in his field - most are still grinding in the 2-4k YouTube follower range.
- Time and money always seem to be short for Sam, and he's constantly got a cup of coffee or a sugar-free Monster in his hand to try and fuel the day. He recently started experimenting with Nootropics as well, but still feels that he's always running on empty.
- Sam finds it hard to discover eco-friendly products in his price range, and although he's doing his best he still doesn't feel like he's reduced his impact enough.

18

BONUS: THE ULTIMATE GUIDE TO RUNNING A BRAINSTORMING SESSION THAT WORKS

"Ideas are cheap and abundant. What is of value is the effective placement of those ideas into situations that develop action."

- Peter Drucker

Brainstorming is a risk. It can be productive, or a big expensive waste of everyone's time.

What's the difference between a good brainstorming session and a bad one?

It comes down to a few things - planning, structure, and preparation. Ironically, something that's supposed to be a freewheeling creative exercise is more productive when it's structured. Why? Because a business brainstorm needs to produce measurable solutions to big, complex problems. If you lay a blank canvas in front of a bunch of middle managers and consultants, you're setting the group up for failure.

A 7-Step Process for Productive Brainstorming Sessions

1. Define - as exactly as possible - the problem you want to solve
2. Before you start identifying solutions, come up with the measures and objectives of the right solution
3. Invite the Right People
4. Set the agenda, aka structure your time
5. Generate initial solutions individually
6. Meet as a group to brainstorm
7. Evaluate your ideas and define next steps

1. Define - as exactly as possible - the problem you want to solve

The first step in any brainstorming session is to define, with exact language, the challenge we're trying to solve. This process will involve setting boundaries for what is and isn't in scope.

For example, let's say you're a car dealer who wants to improve the service booking experience on your website. It would be out of scope to talk about how to enhance employees' phone interactions with customers.

2. Before you start identifying solutions, come up with the measures and objectives of the right solution

This step leads on nicely from defining the challenge and setting boundaries. If, for example, you're that same car dealer and you are brainstorming a new booking experience from the ground up, you'll want to define a good experience

- what goals will this new booking experience help customers achieve?

In her Forbes article, "4 Steps to Successful Brainstorming[1]", Susan Adams describes an example of setting a brainstorming objective:

> "*David Kelley, the founder of renowned design firm I.D.E.O., wanted to design a product that would enable cyclists to transport and drink coffee while they were riding.*
>
> *A couple of ways to describe what he wanted to design: "spill-proof coffee cup lids," or "bicycle cup holders."*
>
> *But a much better description is the following objective: 'helping bike commuters to drink coffee without spilling it or burning their tongues.'"*

3. Invite the Right People

Your brainstorming session needs to include people across many levels and areas of your brand, including:

- Experts on the topic
- People in the company affected by the challenge
- Non-experts such as managers from another part of the business, front-line staff, or non-employees

Diversity of thought, background, age, experience, and perspective is critical, and will only strengthen the solutions the group discovers.

Note: Your brainstorming session will also need a facilitator, which could be you or someone you nominate. The facilitator must be someone who can command a room, keep the session on track, and is unbiased. Often outside consultants who specialize in leading brainstorming sessions are a good choice because they don't have a vested interest in the outcomes.

4. Set the agenda, aka structure your time

Nothing gets people to think on their feet like time constraints. While you'll want to devote some introduction time to warm-up exercises and introductions, you'll also need to make that ideation time is limited.

The meat of the brainstorming session will consist of two sections:

- Idea generation
- Idea evaluation

Although idea generation is what comes to mind when people think "brainstorming," idea evaluation is arguably more important. It helps us better understand what makes a good idea, what will fly in the real world, and what the practical considerations may be for implementation.

If the perfection solution isn't found in the room, idea evaluation will serve as a good template for what works moving forward.

5. Generate initial solutions individually

Two of the biggest problems with brainstorming in a group are:

- The loudest voices tend to overpower the group

decision-making process. Sometimes the best ideas come from people who are less forward with their opinions, and we need to make sure their voices are heard as well.

- When people hear other people's solutions to a problem, they get stuck on that idea. They use it to judge their own potential ideas and the ideas of others. They may not share their ideas because they feel they won't live up to the arbitrary objectives laid out in this first idea.

By giving participants time to think about the problem individually, you're setting up a more productive group session. This way, there'll be enough time to truly consider the issue, and all voices will be heard in the group session.

6. Meet as a group to brainstorm

 "Nothing is original. Steal from anywhere that resonates with inspiration or fuels your imagination.

Authenticity is invaluable; originality is non-existent.

– Jim Jarmusch

Now that you're prepped and the participants have had enough time to consider their solutions, you're ready to meet as a group.

The "idea generation" section of this session is best structured with formal activities.

Below are a few exercises to help warm up the group, or rethink a challenge that might have us stuck.

You don't need to use them in any particular order. Instead, you can pick and choose from the list to see what works best for you.

1. S.C.A.M.P.E.R.

Scamper is a checklist that helps us rethink a problem. It's particularly helpful if you're stuck and need to take a step back. SCAMPER stands for:

- Substitute: This is where you take away an element, concept, or step in a process and replace it with something else. For example, if you're trying to design a better bike, you might consider substituting wood or plastic for metal.
- Combine: Can you combine elements of the challenge to come up with something new? By combining two elements, you can think about your problem in new ways and break out of the usual thinking. For example, the printing press was created when Gutenberg combined two unrelated products: a grape press and a coin punch.
- Adapt: Is there something that's working well for another challenge that might fix your current problem? For example, scientists often look to the natural world to discover a technological solution. The design of sharkskin scales, which allows algae to slide easily off of sharks' skin, has been adapted to catheter technology to help reduce infections.

- Modify: Magnifying or minimizing parts of your challenge can give you a fresh perspective on solving it. For example, can you scale a part of your business to the point where economies of scale work in your favor?
- Put to other use: Is there a way to put current ideas to other uses, in a way that might solve other problems?
- Eliminate: What would happen if you got rid of parts of your product or experience? Would you resolve any issues by simply removing compounding factors and simplifying your customer journey?
- Rearrange: Is there a way to rearrange the sequence, components, timing, or pace of an experience in a way that might enhance the customer journey?

2. Sticky Notes and a Stop Clock

- Post the problem you're trying to solve.
- Hand out a stack of sticky notes to everyone.
- Set a timer for 90 second sand have everyone write down as many solutions to the problem as they can think of. This exercise is quantity over quantity - write down as many ideas as possible.
- After time is up, have everyone read their ideas aloud and group similar ideas on a whiteboard or wall.
- Hold an open group discussion around the most common ideas.

3. 5 Why's

The 5 Whys technique was created by Toyota. It's central to their internal problem-solving framework. Taiichi Ohno[2], described the method as, "the basis of Toyota's scientific approach. By repeating why five times, the nature of the problem as well as its solution becomes clear."

Teams are encouraged to literally ask "why" five times when they see the way something is being done on the factory floor — each time, moving deeper into the underlying cause of assumptions, issues, and processes.

4. The Stepladder Technique

The Stepladder Technique helps make sure that quieter members of the group are heard. Developed by Steven Rogelberg, Janet Barnes-Farrell, and Charles Lowe, it helps avoid groupthink by making sure everyone speaks up before louder members influence them.

The Stepladder Technique best suited to be the first exercise in a brainstorming session. There are five steps in this exercise, some of which need to happen before your group meeting:

- **Step 1:** Before meeting as a big group, send the challenge out to al members. Make sure to give everyone enough time to think about the problem and independently come up with ideas around how to solve.
- **Step 2:** In the meeting, pair off everyone into groups of two for discussion of their ideas.
- **Step 3:** Add in a third group member, who will

share their individual ideas before the group of two shares theirs.

- **Step 4:** Repeat the same process by adding a fourth member, fifth member, etc..
- **Step 5:** Once everyone has presented their ideas, you can discuss as a group and find a consensus on the best next action.

7. Evaluate your ideas and define next steps

After individual, small group, and group brainstorming has finished, everyone will need to come together and evaluate the ideas. And in fact, you'll probably find a lot of overlap. This is where our sticky notes will come in handy, as we'll need to group duplicate ideas on a whiteboard or wall and start to discover narrative threads. Then, we'll need to start deciding which of these solutions are most appropriate.

A whole book could be written about how to constructively evaluate ideas (my favorite being Edward de Bono's Six Thinking Hats[3]). Our previous steps should have helped us define the problem, the scope of our solutions, and the objective that decides whether our solutions are appropriate.

Each organization will have its own measures for what makes an idea practical. However, we do want to make sure that people leave the session with next steps.

A simple but great tool to understand next steps is an Impact Effort Matrix.

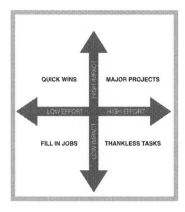

We'll take our sticky note solutions and plot them on the matrix according to how much effort they'll take to accomplish and how much impact the project will make.

This way, we'll be able to define our quick wins. Everyone will leave the session fired-up to get started.

19

BONUS: THREE CRITICAL CHECKLISTS FOR CUSTOMER JOURNEY MAPPING

> *"One essential characteristic of modern life is that we all depend on systems—on assemblages of people or technologies or both—and among our most profound difficulties is making them work."*
> — Atul Gawande, *The Checklist Manifesto*

I n this section, I've included several checklists from Part One that are particularly helpful during the Journey Mapping process. These are also available for download at CXThatSings.com/resources if you'd prefer to download and print PDF versions.

1. Customer Journey Map Basics: A Checklist
2. 10 Key Questions to Answer When Developing a Marketing Persona
3. 10 Key Questions to Answer When Populating the "Do, Think, Stop" Framework

Customer Journey Map Basics: A Checklist

1. Does your Customer Journey Map focus on just one persona?
2. Does it follow the purchase/interaction journey across all sales channels?
3. Does your Customer Journey Map include both mechanical and emotional customer measures (thoughts, feelings, pain points, emotional responses, etc.)?
4. Did you include and indicate key Moments of Truth in your map?
5. Does it contain opportunities for innovation, based off of the pain points and Moments of Truth you identified?

10 Key Questions to Answer When Developing a Marketing Persona

1. Is your core customer male, female or an even mix of both? If even, why did you choose a man or woman as your target (and does it matter)?
2. Is your persona single, married, or co-habitating?
3. Do they have kids now? If so how many and what ages? If not, are they planning on having kids soon?
4. How old are they?
5. What's their income level?
6. How much expendable income do they have to buy your product? Do they have to make trade-offs to be able to afford it?

7. What are their 5 favorite sites, social networks, and brands?

8. If they could describe your customer experience in three words, what would those words be?

9. What kind of environment do they live in? Are they living with roommates, renting, or own their home?

10. What responsibilities and recurring costs do they have? Pets, a car, a mortgage, going out every Saturday night with friends, pedicures, etc.?

10 Key Questions to Answer When Populating the "Do, Think, Stop" Framework

1. Are you stopping at what customers say, or digging into what they are actually doing?

2. Are your answers based on assumptions, or on research and data?

3. Have you identified those key Moments of Truth where your customer is forming their most impactful opinions around your product?

4. Have you looked at non-owned channels, such as retailers that stock your products, Amazon reviews, and Google results?

5. Have you dug into the places where your customers go for reviews, feedback, unboxing, or product previews?

6. If your customers are saying one thing and doing another, can you identify why?

7. Are you treating all your findings as hypotheses, and trying to prove them wrong (instead of right)?

8. Are you a victim of confirmation bias? In other words, are you just seeing the data that confirms what you already believe to be true or are you letting the data tell the story?

9. Have there been any big changes in your customer experience (such as the introduction of new sales channels) that may be impacting your customer's actions?

10. Have you included qualitative as well as quantitative data in your research?

20

BONUS: AVOID THESE 7 DECISION TRAPS BY THINKING LIKE A SCIENTIST

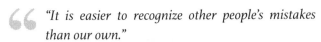 *"It is easier to recognize other people's mistakes than our own."*
— *Daniel Kahneman*

W hat if I told you that making a decision is not a one-off event? Even if you're someone who likes to go with your gut, your "quick" choice is actually the product of a fluid process subject to common errors in thinking.

There are hidden forces in your mind that shape your choices. And these forces aren't random. In fact, they are common, predictable, and easy to spot if you know what you're looking for.

In his book **Predictably Irrational: The Hidden Forces That Shape Our Decisions**, Dan Ariely puts it this way:

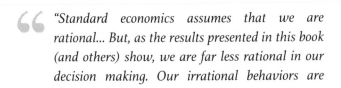 *"Standard economics assumes that we are rational... But, as the results presented in this book (and others) show, we are far less rational in our decision making. Our irrational behaviors are*

> *neither random nor senseless- they are systematic and predictable. We all make the same types of mistakes over and over, because of the basic wiring of our brains."*
> — *Dan Ariely*

You may believe that your decisions are bulletproof. Unfortunately, everyone, from the CEO down to the office intern, is subject to errors in thinking. They're called cognitive biases, and they shape the way we take in, process, and use information. The context of the information we get and the filters we use to consider it are as important as the information itself.

Combating cognitive bias can improve your ROI

In a recent study, McKinsey showed that when companies worked to reduce the effects of cognitive bias, they raised ROI by at least 7%. However, these cognitive biases are hard to spot if you don't know what you're looking for.

Take the time to ask yourself each of these 10 questions to discover if you're falling victim to a common cognitive bias. There's no downside, but the upside on spotting faulty thinking can be huge.

Here's a five minute checklist for detecting cognitive bias

Check for Self-serving Bias

This is the tendency for people to protect their ego and vested interests. It might take the form of cherry-picking data to support your current opinion. You might be dismissing the views of dissenters because you don't want to bruise your ego.

Interrogate the data and assumptions that led to this decision and ask yourself, **"Was anything dismissed because it didn't agree with my vested interest (or my boss')?"**

Check for the Affect Heuristic

This is the tendency for people to make a decision based on their emotional state. For instance, if you emotionally associate "innovation" with something positive, you're more likely to judge a new project as being lower risk than it actually is.

Interrogate your own feelings and associations with this project. Ask yourself honestly, **"Have I fallen in love with this idea?"**

Check for Groupthink

This is the tendency for decision-making groups to favor conformity with the team over making the more rational decision. They don't want to risk being an outcast, so they go along with the herd mentality, resulting in an irrational outcome.

Think through the project and ask yourself, **"Did me, or anyone else on the team, disagree with the majority opinion? Was their voice heard, or was it shouted down in favor of the group?"**

Check for the Halo Effect

This is the tendency to assume lots of ambiguous facts based on one particular point. For instance, if you find someone attractive, you're more likely to think they're honest, competent, and intelligent.

Look at the case studies and facts that led you to this decision. Ask yourself, **"Am I assuming that because a similar approach worked for someone else (who's successful), that it'll work for me?"**

Check for the Sunk-Cost Fallacy

This is the tendency for people to let past time and money costs influence the future of a project. However, future costs of a project are the only rational point of data for investors. This is the bias that leads people to throw "good money after bad."

Ask yourself, **"If I was the new CEO on my first day, would I still make the same decision? Or am I being over-influenced by the history of this project?"**

Check for Overconfidence Bias

This is the tendency for people to think of their own abilities as better than they are because they're successful now. They tend to make every decision with the attitude that they "can't lose," because of their current success.

Ask yourself, **"How skeptical am I? Did I challenge all my assumptions? Am I being overconfident because of my current success?"**

Check for Loss Aversion

This is the tendency for people to want to avoid a loss more than they want to risk an equivalent gain. Often, you'll see this bias in people who don't want to sell a house for less than they paid for it. They'd rather lose money holding out for a higher purchase price than risk getting back less than they paid.

Ask yourself, **"How open to risk am I? Am I picking the safest option because it's the right option, or the least risky?"**

Here are three book recommendations for learning more about Decision Bias and how to avoid it

1. **"Predictably Irrational", written by Dan Arierly:** In this book, the author explores the common assumption that people behave rationally. However, what he found is that people constantly overpay, underestimate, and procrastinate. More to the point, these behaviors aren't random — they're predictable.

2. **"Thinking, Fast and Slow", written by Daniel Kahneman:** In his Nobel Prize-winning work, Kahneman explores how people think, remember, and make decisions. His thesis is that people think in two ways: fast, intuitive thinking, and slow, rational thinking. However, our brains are lazy and usually make whichever decision

requires the least effort. This leads to a reliance on cognitive bias and mental short cuts.

3. **"The Halo Effect", written by Phil Rosenzweig:** This fascinating read delves into the tendency of experts to examine high performing companies, then spread this "golden glow" to all of the company's attributes. But, as the author explains, these experts are "not just wrong, but deluded".

Additional Resources

Key Terms

The Advocacy Process

The least productive and most biased method of decision making. Managers view the decision making process as a competition to dominate, become attached to their personal solution, and cherry-pick data to make a case that will defeat the competition.

The Inquiry Process

The preferred method of decision making. In this process, managers consider a variety of options, weight often conflicting data, and work as a team to discover the best solution.

Self-Serving Bias

This is people's tendency to attribute positive events to themselves but attribute negative events to external, uncontrollable factors. For example, thinking "I was late because traffic was bad, but Jane was late because she's a disorganized person".

Affect Heuristic

This is people's tendency to let their emotions dictate their decisions. This mental short cut is used when weighing risks and benefits of a decision, based on the feelings a person associates with something. If you find yourself "going with your gut" on a decision, you're likely relying on the Affect Heuristic.

Confirmation Bias

This is people's tendency to search for, interpret, choose, and remember data that confirms a preexisting belief. For example, if I don't believe climate change exists and want to build a case for that hypothesis, but then only Google "climate change is fake", I'm exhibiting Confirmation Bias in my research.

Anchoring Bias

This is people's tendency to rely too much on the first piece of information they see when making a decision. For instance, if you read through a qualitative research piece that says your customers have a great in-store experience but that your digital touchpoints are broken, then another that says your digital touchpoints are first-rate, you're more likely to conclude that your digital touchpoints are what you need to work on the most.

Halo Effect

This is the tendency for people to make assumptions about unrelated information based on a concrete piece of information that's immediately noticeable. For instance, it's well documented that people assume attractive and well-dressed people are "better" people when it comes to moral, leadership, or intellectual decisions.

Sunk-Cost Fallacy

This is the tendency for people to over-value the sunk costs i a project (those costs, economic or psychological, that have been spent and are unable to be recovered). In every day speech, this often results in "throwing good money after bad".

Optimism Bias

This is the tendency for people to believe that they (or their team) have a lower risk of experiencing negative event as compared to others. For example, Blockbuster felt they were immune to the competitive threat of Netflix because of prior success. In 2008, Blockbuster CEO Jim Keyes told the Motley Fool, "Neither RedBox nor Netflix are even on the radar screen in terms of competition. It's more Wal-Mart and Apple." Blockbuster filed for bankruptcy in 2010.

Loss Aversion

This describes people's tendency to prefer avoiding a loss versus acquiring an equivalent gain. For example, people would prefer not to lose $20 that's already in their pockets as compared to finding $20 on the street. This is because they overvalue the "bird in hand" as compared to a potential, but not promised, gain.

21

BONUS: THE PSYCHOLOGY OF AN UNFORGETTABLE CUSTOMER EXPERIENCE

87% of organizations say traditional experiences no longer satisfy customers.

So how do you build a CX that stands out from the crowd?

> *"People will forget what you said, people will forget what you did, but people will never forget how you made them feel."*
> — *Maya Angelou*

The problem with a traditional customer experience

According to Accenture[1], 87% of organizations say traditional experiences no longer satisfy customers. A "good" experience is ok, but for your brand to break through with customers, it needs to stand out.

An unforgettable experience means customers talk about it. They recommend it, and prefer it. In short, **being unforgettable drives your bottom line.**

The science behind creating an unforgettable customer experience

How do we create an experience that stands out?

First, it helps to understand how our brains create memories.

Nobel Prize-winning economist Daniel Kahneman explored this subject in a study about how people remember pain[2]. He asked people to rate their discomfort of colonoscopy procedure. Kahneman's team then compared the patients' "remembered" pain experiences with data recorded during the procedure.

To their surprise, the team found people rated the pain of the entire experience based on only two points: The intensity of pain at its worst point, and the pain at the end of the procedure.

Kahneman discovered that our brains can't remember everything, so they use mental shortcuts (called heuristics) to pick out what's important.

One of the most important heuristics is emotion— the **more intense and more recent the feelings, the more memorable the experience.**

These findings are the foundation of the psychology principle known as the **Peak-end Rule.**

The Peak-End Rule and what it means for brands

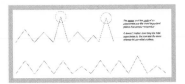

The Peak-end Rule says that people judge an experience based on how they felt at its peak and its end, not the average of every moment of the experience. And that's true whether the experience was good or bad.

For brands, this means customers will remember their whole experience based on only two moments—the best (or worst) part of their experience, and the end.

That's great news because, according to science, there's room for error in your experience. To transform people's memories of your brand, you only have to perfect two moments—the peak and end.

Examples of brands that use the Peak-end Rule to perfection

1. Chick-fil-A: The human drive-thru

The drive-thru can be a stressful place. You're not quite sure what you want, there's pressure from the cars behind you, and you're afraid your order will be wrong when you finally get your food.

Chick-fil-A has eliminated the most stressful points of the drive-thru by introducing humans. The crew members:

- Come to you (reducing time pressure from other cars)
- You can ask them questions (no more worry about the accuracy of your order)
- They end every interaction with the delightful Chick-fil-A trademark phrase, "It's my pleasure."

2. Aldi: Home to the world's fastest checkout

At the discount grocery chain Aldi, you won't find fancy displays or ornate decorations. The shelves are ugly metal racks stacked with mostly store-brand products. But the most memorable part of Aldi? It's lightning fast check-out process.

Aldi has long been home to the world's fastest checkouts—a huge pain point (and emotional low) in most grocery stores. But because Aldi sells owned-brand products, they can create packaging with multiple UPCs on different panels. Cashiers never have to search for where to scan, rarely look up an item code. They're even scored based on the length of their average checkout.

Aldi has turned an industry pain point into an opportunity to create an unforgettable customer experience.

3. Zappos: Fast and free returns

The secret to Zappos' success lies in how they handle the number one challenge of buying shoes online—what do you do if they don't fit? Because of their liberal return policy, Zappos quickly built a thriving business.

In this case, the peak and end of an experience are tied to the same moment—returning an item. Knowing that Zappos happily takes returns created brand advocates, drove trial, and increased repeat customers.

Why is it important to create an unforgettable experience?

The Peak-End Rule is like the 80/20 shortcut of customer experience. 20% of your experience drives 80% of what people's memories of the experience. And the more unforgettable the experience, the better the customer:

- **They're loyal.** Customers who had a "very good" experience are 3.5x more likely to repurchase. According to Temkin Group's 2018 research[3], CX has three components—success, effort, and emotion. They state, "while all three elements impact customer loyalty, an improvement in *emotion* drives the most significant increase in loyalty."
- **They're advocates.** Customers who had a good experience are 5x more likely to recommend the company. In fact, "there's a 21-point difference in Net Promoter Score between consumers who've had a very good experience with a company and those who've had a very poor experience." (Temkin Group)
- **They drive revenue.** Temkin also built a model to estimate how "a modest improvement in CX would impact the revenue of a typical $1 billion company across in 20 industries." On average, these companies stand to gain $775 million in value over only three years.

The bottom line

CX projects take a lot of time, money, and sweat equity to complete. They're rarely small and always cross departments. That means lots of stakeholders, which translates to lots of resistance.

But the beautiful thing about Peak-end is that you can start applying it to your strategy today.

Find the biggest pain point in your customer journey. Attack it, and you won't just improve that moment, you'll enhance your entire experience.

22

BONUS: CHOICE OVERLOAD - WHY SIMPLICITY IS THE KEY TO WINNING CUSTOMERS

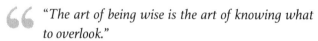 *"The art of being wise is the art of knowing what to overlook."*
— *William James*

Have you ever experienced analysis paralysis? It's that feeling of anxiety when you have so much information that any action feels like the wrong one, so you don't do anything at all.

As marketers, we often assume that giving people more information is better. But to customers, more options can be paralyzing.

Too many choices will overwhelm, but just enough will drive sales

In a famous study[1] conducted at Columbia University, a research team set up a booth of jam samples. Every few hours they would switch from a selection of 24 jams to a group of six jams.

When there were 24 jams, 60% of customers would stop

to get a sample, and 3% of these customers would buy a jar. When there were six jams on display, only 40% stopped. But here's the interesting part—30% of these people bought jam.

Lots of options attracted customers to browse, but fewer choices got them to buy.

Are you losing sales by giving customers too much choice?

The negative effects of choice can be more severe than a missed sale. Research shows that when there are too many options, customers feel anxious, will disengage, and can even become depressed.

The adverse effects of too much choice is down to a behavioral science principle known as Choice Overload. It's the idea that while some choice can be good, too much choice will overwhelm customers.

A brand's good intentions—giving customers lots of options—can backfire and become a barrier to sales.

According to recent research from Episerver, 46% of customers have failed to complete a purchase online due to overwhelming choices.

How people choose—the Paradox of Choice

In his book "The Paradox of Choice," Schwartz outlines the steps of decision making:

- Figure out your goals
- Evaluate the importance of each goal
- Array the options according to how well they meet each goal

- Evaluate the how likely each of the options is to meet your goals
- Pick the winning option

The problem is, the more options you have, the harder it is to make a comparison across products. If you have to compare an item across 50 dimensions instead of 3, there's a risk you're missing out on "the one."

That's the paradox—having a variety of options is good. It drives customer consideration. But once the number of choices gets too high, a person's happiness goes down.

The curse of too many options

1. Anxiety

Too much choice is the cause of mental anguish for some people. Economist Herman Simon theorized that decision-making styles fall into two types:

Satisficers

People who would rather make an "ok decision" than the perfect decision. They've spent some time considering their options, but haven't belabored the process. They tend to be more satisfied with their choice because they don't consider all the available information.

Satisficers settle for an option that's "good enough" and move on. Gretchen Rubin, author of "The Happiness Project" described them this way:

"*Satisficers* *make a decision once their criteria are met; when they find the hotel or the pasta sauce that has the qualities they want, they're satisfied."*

Maximizers

These are people who want to make the best possible decision . They can't choose until they've deeply examined every possible option.

Research from Swarthmore College found that Maximizers reported significantly less life satisfaction, happiness, optimism, and self-esteem. They also experienced much higher levels of and regret and depression than Satisficers.

2. Disappointment

The more options people have, more likely they are to be disappointed in their choice. You never feel that you made the best decision because there were too many options to consider.

As Barry Schwartz writes in The Paradox of Choice:

*"The existence of multiple alternatives makes it easy for us to imagine alternatives that don't exist—alternatives that combine the attractive features of the ones that do exist. And to the extent that we engage our imaginations in this way, we will be even less satisfied with the alternative we end up choosing. So, once again, **a greater variety of choices actually makes us feel worse.**"*

Combat Choice Overload with these strategies

- **Offer fewer options:** It may seem counterintuitive in the age of personalization, options need to be limited to maximize sales. For example, Procter & Gamble found that a decrease in the number of Head & Shoulders varieties resulted in a 10% increase in revenue.

- **Make it easy to compare features across products:** If you want to make it easy for customers to choose between non-equal options, frame the use of each. For example, many software companies use Basic, Premium, and Pro options to reduce the number of choices. Then, they compare features across products in a table that's clear and easy to digest. Now instead of feeling confused and anxious about which version to pick, customers can easily choose the product that's right for the features they need.

The bottom line

There's no silver bullet in marketing, but it's common to see brands undermining their efforts with good intentions.

If you reduce the number of options available, you also reduce complexity for the customer.

In the end, it's this reduction in complexity that will smooth the way to increased consideration, higher engagement, and more sales.

It takes a brave marketer to suggest a company reduce their product portfolio, but ask yourself, "If this is something that's worked so well for so many brands, isn't it at least worth a test?".

23

BONUS: WHY PERSONALIZING YOUR CUSTOMER EXPERIENCE WILL MAKE IT IRRESISTIBLE TO CUSTOMERS

> *"Personalization is pointless without knowing the individual. Understand the dreams, hopes, and fears that motivate your customers, then hit them where it counts."*
>
> *– Paul Gillin*

I t seems like every brand is chasing personalization. In fact, almost 70% of companies surveyed in a recent Everstring report[1] called it a "top priority."

It could be easy to write personalization off as a shiny object, if not for the financial returns.

In their 2019 Personalization Development Study[2], Monetate outlined the ROI of personalized marketing:

- **Personalized marketing drives growth:** 93% of companies with an "advanced personalization strategy" saw revenue growth. Only 45.4% of companies without a personalization strategy saw equivalent growth.

- **The higher the investment, the better the returns:** Companies with ROI of 2x or more said personalization made up at least 20% of their marketing budget.
- **Personalization drives long-term customer value:** Brands that had the highest personalization ROI (3x or more) focused on loyalty as their top KPI. Companies with lower ROI targeted short term measures like average order value.

It's clear there's evidence supporting personalization. It compels customers to act, and they're actively asking for more. In a recent study[3], Infosys found that 31% of customers wish their experiences were "far more" personalized.

But why?

The answer lies in a psychological principle known as the **Cocktail Party Effect.**

What is the Cocktail Party Effect?

The Cocktail Party Effect was discovered in the 1950s by a British Cognitive scientist named Colin Cherry.

Cherry wanted to understand what people focus on and why. After researching the dynamics of a noisy room, he discovered something interesting. Our brain separates overlapping conversations into different auditory streams. It can then decide to ignore information that isn't relevant.

How do our brains decide what information to pay attention to?

The Cocktail Party Effect states that people focus on information relevant to them. According to a recent study,[4] a key trigger for "tuning in" is when people hear their name.

Given the research, it makes sense that brands start personalization efforts with a customer's name. But the Cocktail Party Effect shows **if we go deeper, relevant content can drive incredible results.**

What is "true personalization"?

Personalization isn't about getting your customer's first name right then spamming them with impersonal ads. As Seth Godin says:

"*[Personalization] is a chance to **differentiate at a human scale**, to use behavior as the most important clue about what people want and more important, what they need.*"

True personalization is deeply understanding your customer's journey. Once you know what they need, you can serve them the right message at the right time, and drive business results.

How to apply the Cocktail Party Effect to your customer experience

1. Get specific about your customer's world

In a recent study, Accenture found[5] the personalization tactics that have a direct effect on buying behaviour:

- **Know my name:** 56% of customers would rather

buy from a retailer that recognizes them
by name.

- **Know my past:** 65% of customers prefer to buy
from a retailer who "knows their purchase
history."
- **Know what I want:** 58% of customers prefer to
buy from a retailer that recommends options
based on their past purchases.

Here's an example of the Cocktail Party Effect in action:

In this email from jewelry brand Monica Vinader, the brand uses customer data in a smart way.

They've not only customized Kim's name in the email ("Made for You Kim"). They've also used images of "K" monogrammed jewelry, and shown a necklace based on Kim's past purchases.[6]

2. Personalize your marketing's visuals, copy, and message

In their 2018 Ecommerce Quarterly Report[7], Monetate discovered that just **three pages of personalized content can double conversion rates**.

Monetate also found that **the value of personalization compounds with each experience.**

True personalization does more than increase purchases. According to Monetate's research, it also gets people to add items to their cart more often and drives down cart abandonment rates.

3. Go deeper with data — and be transparent

Your ability to personalize effectively is directly tied to the state of your brand's data.

And if the data is there, but it isn't in shape, getting to the right insights might mean digging a little deeper. Further research could take the form of progressive profiling, marketing automation, or just asking your customers if the marketing they're getting is right for them.

Another example of the Cocktail Party Effect in action:

EasyJet, a British low-cost airline, made a company milestone relevant for their customers.

Instead of making their 20th anniversary about the brand, EasyJet focused on the consumer. They transformed people's data into a celebration of their travels with EasyJet[8]:

The bottom line

Personalization might be a top priority for brands, but most haven't achieved their ambitions.

And that's a problem because, according to Gartner[9], the stakes are high. In a recent survey, they discovered brands are at risk of losing 38% of their customers because of poor personalization.

There's no magic button you can press to become immediately personalized. It's a tough process that requires marketers to work closely with IT, operations, and digital teams.

But at the end of the day, the potential for revenue generation is huge. The science supports it, and customers are asking for it.

So instead of asking if you should focus on personalization, the better question is, "How can we prioritize it?"

24

BONUS: CUSTOMER EXPERIENCE CASE STUDY - AMAZON

HOW AMAZON USES PSYCHOLOGY TO DRIVE SALES

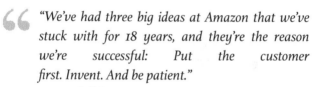

"We've had three big ideas at Amazon that we've stuck with for 18 years, and they're the reason we're successful: Put the customer first. Invent. And be patient."
— *Jeff Bezos*

Amazon seems to be the Terminator of eCommerce — they're ever-evolving, learning, and growing. Because so many people shop at Amazon, they're able to test on a massive scale, which gives them the benefit of learning on a massive scale as well.

So it's no surprise that when it comes to driving sales, few brands do it better than Amazon.

However, you may be surprised to learn that there are psychological and behavioral economics principles underlying their most effective sales tactics.

5 psychological principles that Amazon uses to drive sales

1. The Peak-end Principle

This principle states that people remember an experience based on how they felt at its most intense point and at its end, instead of the average of every moment.

How does Amazon apply Peak-end?

Amazon applies the Peak-end Principle by taking the friction out of the two most significant eCommerce pain points — payments and shipping.

When Amazon has your card on file, payments are invisible. You can simply click "Buy Now," and the product is on its way to your house.

For Prime members, shipping is a breeze as well. One of the primary benefits of Prime is "free" and fast shipping. Prime takes the friction out of waiting for your order to arrive and makes the online channel more attractive than the same product in a store.

2. The Reciprocity Principle

Reciprocity is a social norm of responding to a positive action with another positive action. It's why you feel indebted when someone does you a favor.

Made famous by Robert Cialdini in his book, "Influence: The Psychology of Persuasion", Reciprocity can be summed with the old adage, "You have to give to get."

For example, in one of Cialdini's studies[1], customers

were 42% more likely to make a purchase if they got a free piece of chocolate when entering a store.

How does Amazon apply the Reciprocity Principle?

One example of using Reciprocity to drive sales is in their Kindle store.Customers can get a peek at a potential purchase's contents using the "Look Inside!" feature.

Because Amazon (and the authors) have essentially given you a free gift by letting you read part of the book, you feel indebted. Now you're more likely to purchase this item because you want to return the favor.

3. Scarcity

The Scarcity Principle states that humans place a higher value something that's scarce, and a lower value on abundantly available things. In his book, Influence, Robert Cialdini described it this way:

"When our freedom to have something is limited, the item becomes less available, and we experience an increased desire for it.

*However, we rarely recognize that psychological reactance has caused us to want the item more; **all we know is that we want it.**"*

How does Amazon apply the Scarcity Principle?

Amazon uses scarcity to its advantage in multiple ways. Their "Deal of the Day," as seen below, implies that these deals are so good, they're only available for 24 hours. People see them as scarce, and therefore even better deals than they are.

Amazon also employs scarcity in it's Woot! section. This offer not only features a ticking clock, it also has limited stock. Now customers feel it's an even scarcer deal (and therefore, more attractive).

4. The Authority Principle

The Authority Principle states that people tend to comply with those in positions of power, such as police, government leaders, professors, and perceived experts.

How does Amazon apply the Authority Principle?

Amazon applies the Authority Principle[2] to its customer experience when people are most overwhelmed by choice, and therefore need help making a decision. During the "browsing" phase, results labeled "Amazon's Choice" appears in almost every category.

Customers, excited by but overwhelmed by the available choice, assume that if anyone knows which products are best, it's Amazon.

In their Editorial recommendations, Amazon provides in-search information from third parties that help customers decide which product in a given category was reviewed as "the best."

So if they don't trust customer reviews, and they think that Amazon's Choice product choices are a little biased, that's ok. They still have an expert giving them advice. Customers don't even have to leave their browser window to snag it.

5. Defaults

In behavioral economics, default options[3] are pre-set actions that take effect if customers don't opt-out. Since defaults don't require people to take any effort, they can be a simple but powerful sales tool.

How does Amazon use Defaults?

Amazon's "Subscribe and Save" feature is a powerful use of defaults. By offering customers a small discount in exchange for creating a recurring subscription, Amazon makes it a customer's default to repurchase the item.

Not only that, but "Subscribe and Save" is pre-selected, so even the process of subscribing is a default. A customer has to think harder to purchase the item once than to buy it multiple times.

The bottom line

There's no doubt that a large part of Amazon's revenue comes from applying these principles. In fact, in 2013, McKinsey estimated[4] that 35% of what customers were buying on Amazon was driven by their suggestive selling algorithms alone.

However, these powerful tactics weren't discovered in a day. They are the product of years of testing and optimization.

That's why, if you want to apply these principles to your brand, a testing mentality is critical. You have to be willing to test the application of the same principle in hundreds of ways.

At Amazon, this willingness comes from the top-down.

> *"If you double the number of experiments you do per year you're going to double your inventiveness."*
> — *Jeff Bezos*

Because Bezos puts his faith in experiments, Amazon rigorously tests these principles and tweaks them until they are revenue-generating machines.

25

BONUS: CUSTOMER EXPERIENCE CASE STUDY - STARBUCKS

HOW STARBUCKS USES PSYCHOLOGY TO CREATE AN UNFORGETTABLE CUSTOMER EXPERIENCE

> *"Starbucks has a role and a meaningful relationship with people that is not only about the coffee."*
> — *Howard Schultz*

Like Amazon, Starbucks has created a powerful customer experience by understanding their customer journey. They've then injected tactics into the experience that drive customers to come back for more.

5 psychological principles that Starbucks uses to create an unforgettable customer experience

1. Cocktail Party Effect

The Cocktail Party Effect states that people focus on information relevant to them. According to a study published in the journal Brain Research[1], a key trigger for "tuning in" is when people hear their name.

Given the research, it makes sense that brands start personalization efforts with a customer's name.

How does Starbucks apply the Cocktail Party Effect?

By asking for a customer's name and writing it on the cup, Starbucks drives love for its brand through a more personalized experience.

2. The Peak-end Principle

This principle states that people remember an experience based on how they felt at its most intense point and at its end, instead of the average of every moment.

How does Starbucks apply Peak-end?

Starbucks applies the Peak-end Principle by removing the two biggest pain points: waiting to pay and waiting for your coffee.

Through its "order ahead" feature, the Starbucks app lets customers skip both the payment and the coffee collection lines. So now, what were two painful moments in the customer journey are completely avoided in favor of a fast and seamless experience.

Starbucks store manager Jesse Wenkoff-White described it this way.

 "We can have fairly long lines in the morning and it's such an awesome option for customers looking to run in and out if they're running late.

I've had so many people tell me how convenient and easy it is.

Our customers that use it absolutely love it."

3. Decoy Effect

The Decoy Effect describes how price comparisons between products affect choice. When there are only two options, and they're priced "fairly," people make decisions according to personal preference.

But, if there's a third choice that's overpriced compared to the first two options, it changes how people consider all options. The third option is a "decoy" choice.

The decoy's purpose is to change perceptions of the other options, not sell.

How does Starbucks apply the Decoy Effect?

Their classic three-tiered sizing structure is a dead giveaway. Starbucks uses this strategic pricing technique so that customers choose the size that provides the most profit to the company.

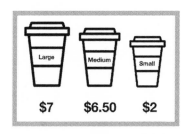

4. Loss Aversion

First identified by Nobel Prize-winner Daniel Kahneman, Loss Aversion is a psychological principle that says people will go to great lengths to avoid losing.

In fact, the psychological pain of losing is twice as powerful[2] as the pleasure of winning.

Because it's so powerful, Loss Aversion features heavily in cognitive psychology and decision theory. It's also one of the most effective tactics[3] for getting customers to buy (the other being Social Proof).

Loss aversion has also been called FOMO — the Fear of Missing Out. It makes people fear they're being left out of exciting events and losing out on the fun.

How does Starbucks take advantage of Loss Aversion?

Starbucks is famous for its limited-edition drinks, such as the Pumpkin Spice Latte and Unicorn Frappuccino, creating devoted brand fans.

Their seasonal traditions loved, many have become cultural landmarks. For example, their festive red Christmas cups herald the true beginning of the holiday season in the U.S.

The flip side of making cups a cultural landmark is creating a sense of FOMO for people who haven't gotten their hands on a limited availability drink. It drives people in-store and makes them feel like they're part of something exclusive and special.

5. Irrational Value Assessment

This principle is taken from the field of behavioral economics. It says that people are irrational when it comes to what an item is worth, and they don't value products objectively.

For example, in Robert Cialdini's classic book, "Influence", he describes a case study where a higher price caused people to buy something more. A jeweler's assistant accidentally doubled the price of every piece of turquoise jewelry in the store. Up to the point, the turquoise had been impossible to sell.

After doubling the price, it sold out in a matter of days.

Why? Because people assumed that because it was so expensive in comparison to the other jewelry, the turquoise must be more valuable. If people see a high-priced item, they automatically assume it's of a higher quality than something more cheaply priced.

How does Starbucks take advantage of Irrational Value Assessment?

Starbucks has taken this powerful psychological technique straight to the bank. By charging more for what used to be a commodity product and dressing it in a premium customer experience, they've revolutionized the entire coffee market.

Their pricing impact has been so huge, it's been dubbed the "Starbucks Effect".

Authors Vijay Vishwanath and David Harding put it this way in their Harvard Business Review[4] article defining the effect:

 "Ten years ago, only 3% of all coffee... was

priced at a premium — at least 25% higher than value brands.

Today, 40% of coffee is sold at premium prices."

— Harvard Business Review, "The Starbucks Effect"

The bottom line

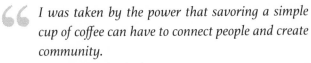

I was taken by the power that savoring a simple cup of coffee can have to connect people and create community.
-Howard Schultz

There's no doubt that a large part of Starbucks revenue comes from applying these psychological principles to their customer experience. In fact, by making Starbucks the so-called "third place" (the other two being home and work), they've managed to open more than 30,000[5] successful stores.

However, these powerful tactics weren't discovered in a day. They are the product of years of testing and optimization.

That's why, if you want to apply these principles to your brand, a testing mentality is critical. You have to be willing to test the application of the same principle in hundreds of ways.

So the only question that remains is, where will you start?

ABOUT THE AUTHOR

Jennifer Clinehens is a CX strategist who's worked both brand and agency-side across North America, Australia, Asia, the U.K., and Europe. Currently, she's the Head of Customer Experience at The Marketing Store in London. Her client-side experience includes time spent as an entrepreneur and Senior Manager at AT&T.

Ms. Clinehens has also lent her strategic expertise to companies like Adidas, Coca-Cola, Delta Airlines, Marks and Spencer (Europe), Westpac (Australia) Colgate-Palmolive, Unilever and McDonald's (U.S., U.K., and Europe).

After a long career as a professional musician and entrepreneur, Jen made a full-time career change to marketing, writing, and speaking in 2011.

Ms. Clinehens is available for speaking, lecturing, and additional writing opportunities. If you'd like to get in touch, please reach out via LinkedIn or connect through email at Jennifer.Clinehens@gmail.com .

ENDNOTES

Introduction

1. Havas Meaningful Brands Study, referenced in MediaPost article "Havas Expands 'Meaningful Brands,' Studies Role Content Plays -- Or Not"; August 2018 https://www.mediapost.com/publications/article/323024/havas-expands-meaningful-brands-studies-role-co.html
2. Bain and Company, "Closing the Delivery Gap" James Allen, Frederick F. Reichheld, Barney Hamilton and Rob Markey; 2005 http://www2.bain.com/bainweb/pdfs/cms/hotTopics/closingdeliverygap.pdf

1. The Customer Empathy Gap

1. McKinsey and Co. "The growth engine: Superior customer experience in insurance" by Tanguy Catlin, Ewan Duncan, Harald Fanderl, and Johannes-Tobias Lorenz. April 2016 https://www.mckinsey.com/industries/financial-services/our-insights/the-growth-engine-superior-customer-experience-in-insurance
2. Bain and Company, "Closing the Delivery Gap" James Allen, Frederick F. Reichheld, Barney Hamilton and Rob Markey; 2005 http://www2.bain.com/bainweb/pdfs/cms/hotTopics/closingdeliverygap.pdf
3. Trinity Mirror Solutions: 'Why we shouldn't trust our gut instinct' Andrew Tenzer, Ian Murray; https://www.trinitymirrorsolutions.co.uk/sites/default/files/2018-07/TMS%20Why%20We%20Shouldn%27t%20Trust%20Our%20Gut%20Instinct%20White%20Paper.pdf

3. Marketing Personas

1. The "Buyer Persona Institute" can be found at http://www.buyerpersona.com/
2. *Totally hypothetical use case and numbers.*
3. *"Buyer Personas: How to Gain Insight into your Customer's Expectations, Align your Marketing Strategies, and Win More Business", by Adele Revella;* https://amzn.to/2w5tZNF
4. "Don't Trust Your Gut", Eric Bonabeau, Harvard Business Review, May 2003; https://hbr.org/2003/05/dont-trust-your-gut

4. Think, Do, Stop

1. Daniel Kahneman, "The riddle of experience vs. memory" Ted2010 https://www.ted.com/talks/daniel_kahneman_the_riddle_of_experience_vs_memory?language=en
2. Fredrickson, Barbara L., and Daniel Kahneman. "Duration neglect in retrospective evaluations of affective episodes." *Journal of personality and social psychology* 65.1 (1993): 45.

5. The Emotional Journey

1. Wilhelm, P., Schoebi, D., and Perrez, M. (2004). Frequency estimates of emotions in everyday life from a diary method's perspective: A comment on Scherer et al.' s survey–study "Emotions in everyday life." Social Science Information 43 (4): 647– 665.
2. Fredrickson, Barbara L., and Daniel Kahneman. "Duration neglect in retrospective evaluations of affective episodes." *Journal of personality and social psychology* 65.1 (1993): 45.
3. Plutchik, R. (1991). The Emotions, 236., Lanham, MD: University Press of America.
4. Measures of emotion: A review; Iris B. Mauss and Michael D. Robinson, https://www.ncbi.nlm.nih.gov/pmc/articles/PMC2756702/

11. Step 5 - Identify opportunities based on your research

1. *The Brainstorming Myth*, Paul A. Mongeau; Annual Meeting of the

Western States Communication Association, 1993. https://archive.org/stream/ERIC_ED357399/ERIC_ED357399_djvu.txt
2. "Seven steps to better brainstorming", Kevin P. Coyne and Shawn T. Coyne; McKinsey Quarterly, 2011.

18. Bonus: The Ultimate Guide to Running a Brainstorming Session That Works

1. Adams, S. (2013, March 6). 4 Steps to Successful Brainstorming. Retrieved from https://www.forbes.com/sites/susanadams/2013/03/05/4-steps-to-successful-brainstorming/#716119275992
2. Ōno, T. (1988). Toyota production system: Beyond large-scale production. Cambridge, Mass: Productivity Press.
3. Bono, E. D. (2017). *Six thinking hats*. London: Penguin Life, an imprint of Penguin Books.

21. Bonus: The psychology of an unforgettable customer experience

1. CMO.com, March 2019; https://www.cmo.com/features/articles/2019/3/11/digital-transformation-20-customer-experience-management.html
2. "Patients' memories of painful medical treatments: real-time and retrospective evaluations of two minimally invasive procedures.", Kahnamen and Redelmeier; https://www.ncbi.nlm.nih.gov/pubmed/8857625
3. "ROI of Customer Experience", 2018; https://temkingroup.com/product/roi-customer-experience-2018/

22. Bonus: Choice Overload - Why simplicity is the key to winning customers

1. *"Too Many Choices: A Problem That Can Paralyze"*, Alina Tugend; *New York Times*, 2010. https://www.nytimes.com/2010/02/27/your-money/27shortcuts.html

23. Bonus: Why personalizing your customer experience will make it irresistible to customers

1. Everstring Report, 69% of Companies Rate Personalizing the Customer Experience as Top in Priority. https://v12data.com/blog/69-companies-rate-personalizing-customer-experience-top-priority/
2. Monetate 2019 Personalization Development Study, https://info.monetate.com/2019-personalization-study.html
3. "Rethinking Retail: Insights from consumers and retailers into an omni-channel customer experience", Infosys; https://www.infosys.com/newsroom/press-releases/Documents/genome-research-report.pdf
4. "The cocktail-party problem revisited: early processing and selection of multi-talker speech", https://www.ncbi.nlm.nih.gov/pmc/articles/PMC4469089/
5. "Consumers Want Personalization: Stats Roundup", https://www.business2community.com/consumer-marketing/consumers-want-personalization-stats-roundup-01694184
6. Campaign Monitor, https://www.campaignmonitor.com/blog/email-marketing/2017/12/8-brands-using-email-personalization-like-pros/
7. Monetate Ecommerce Quarterly Report, 2018; https://info.monetate.com/rs/092-TQN-434/images/EQ4%202018%20-%20Progressing%20With%20Personalization.pdf
8. Campaign Monitor, https://www.campaignmonitor.com/blog/email-marketing/2017/12/8-brands-using-email-personalization-like-pros/
9. "Gartner Survey Shows Brands Risk Losing 38 Percent of Customers Because of Poor Marketing Personalization Efforts"; https://www.gartner.com/en/newsroom/press-releases/2019-03-11-gartner-survey-shows-brands-risk-losing-38-percent-of

24. Bonus: Customer Experience Case Study - Amazon

1. Cialdini, R. B. (2007). Influence: The psychology of persuasion.
2. Source: NN Group, https://www.nngroup.com/articles/authority-principle/
3. Source: Behavioral Economics.com, https://www.behavioraleconomics.com/resources/mini-encyclopedia-of-be/default-optionsetting/
4. "How retailers can keep up with consumers", Ian MacKenzie, Chris Meyer, and Steve Noble, October 2013; https://www.mckinsey.com/in-

dustries/retail/our-insights/how-retailers-can-keep-up-with-consumers

25. Bonus: Customer Experience Case Study - Starbucks

1. "The cocktail-party problem revisited: early processing and selection of multi-talker speech", Bronkhorst; https://www.ncbi.nlm.nih.gov/pmc/articles/PMC4469089
2. Kahneman & Tversky, 1979; https://www.behavioraleconomics.com/resources/mini-encyclopedia-of-be/loss-aversion/
3. "How Loss Aversion and Conformity Threaten Organizational Change", Sean Ryan; https://hbr.org/2016/11/how-loss-aversion-and-conformity-threaten-organizational-change
4. "The Starbucks Effect", Vijay Vishwanath and David Harding; https://hbr.org/2000/03/the-starbucks-effect
5. "Starbucks is modernizing its stores", Danielle Wiener-Bronner, March 2019; https://edition.cnn.com/2019/03/20/business/starbucks-store-renovations/index.html

Made in the
USA
Columbia, SC